The Women's Survival Guide

~ Back to Basics ~

To Barbara ~
Thank you for your support, advice, and precious friendship! ~ Lisa Creedon

The Women's Survival Guide

~ Back to Basics ~

By

Lisa Creedon

Bookstand Publishing
www.BookstandPublishing.com

Published by
Bookstand Publishing
Gilroy, CA 95020
2016_21

ISBN 978-1-58909-353-9

Printed in the United States of America

Table of Contents

Acknowledgments

*This book is dedicated to the Glory of God, through whom
all things are possible, to my husband, Terry,
for always believing in me, and to
Lindsay and Leslie, our precious daughters,
who have made our lives complete.*

~~~~~~~

*If we are fortunate, we have people in our lives who are strong
when we need their strength and always willing when we
need their help. I want to thank my family and friends
for the strength and continuing support
they have so freely given:*

*Martha & James Wood, Doris McCloskey,
Myron & Emily Martin, Steve & Marie Watson,
Dr. Cindy Bristow, Stan Davis, Cille Allen,
Travis Prather, D.A. Gruno, Carol McDonough,
Leslie Raab, Shirley Wilson, Nada Long,
Dawn Crouch, and Lynn Beacham.*

*Special thanks to Barbara Cone, Suzanne Lunsford,
Candice Thompson, Rev. Leigh Martin,
Deborah Burford, Mary Katherine Legg,
and Joe & Kay Legg.*

*Thanks also to the great staff of Bookstand Publishing,
especially Kari and Emily, for their support,
counsel, and assistance.*

Whatever is true, whatever is noble,
whatever is right, whatever is pure,
whatever is lovely, whatever is admirable –
if anything is excellent or praiseworthy –
think about such things.
Phillippians4:8

Chapter One
Finding Happiness
Commit to the Lord whatever you do, and your plans will succeed.
Proverbs 16:3

For some of us, happiness is like an elusive butterfly that flits about, sometimes landing on our shoulder, sometimes fluttering just beyond our reach. When we are happy, we feel better. We feel healthier, smarter. There is a bounce in our step. Our shoulders are back and our heads are held a little higher. We greet challenges with confidence.

That is where we *want* to be and where we *need* to be. Happy people have fewer health problems. And they generally have fewer relationship problems. Why? Because happy people want others to be happy too!

Do you know that true happiness comes from within? That you are responsible for your state of happiness? Each day, you can choose to be happy or sad. If you always depend on others to make you happy, you will frequently be disappointed.

When challenges arise, what happens? Do you worry constantly? Do you pray? Do you keep repeating, "Not another problem! All I have is bad luck!" Stop for a moment and think about your focus. When you are upset, your focus is on being upset.

To make positive changes, you must focus on positive thoughts. Say, "What can I do? I'm afraid!!!" several times. Say it anxiously while you are thinking of a bad situation. Now, speak calmly: "I know things are going to improve. Everything will work out for the best. I am at peace." Can you feel yourself becoming calmer and more relaxed?

When we focus on negative things, we stay in a frantic state of mind. This does not allow us to work toward a positive solution. While we might be seeking a physical solution (immediate cash, job, home, etc.), we are also seeking what we think will make us happy.

Some folks choose to whine. It is a case of the "If only's...." If only I had a husband, if only I were single, if only I had a better job, if only my husband had a better job, if only I had a better car/house, if only my kids were older/younger/more respectful, if only I felt better, if only I had more money, and so on.

While some of these things might provide temporary happiness, true happiness (and the right answers) comes from inner peace. Once you are at peace, you will be able to take responsibility and make positive decisions. Carefully consider your choices. Sometimes you must make a major life change to find your peace. And let God always be first in your life.

Needs and Wants: be careful not to let money control you. Do not let lack of money turn you into a bitter person who people want to avoid. If you keep God first, truly trust Him, and truly believe He will never forsake you, then you also believe and trust He will provide for *all your needs.* The key word is *need.* We know that *needs* are different from *wants.* If we are not careful, a bad case of *wants* can steal our happiness.

Our *wants* are sometimes fed by charge cards. If you are in debt and have needs, try to save until you can pay cash. Try not to use cards for routine purchases. Increasing your debt/monthly payments can also increase your stress level and overall unhappiness.

If Mama Ain't Happy, Ain't Nobody Happy

I love that saying. It is so true. When I am sad, it affects the entire family. Everyone gathers around, full of sympathy and offers of what they could do to make me feel better. Of course, that is for short-term sadness. If we reach a point where we are always sad (depression), what happens? Others start to avoid us. They don't want to be dragged down into our pit of despair. Friends disappear. At that point, concern from your family might be limited to whether there is anything to eat and if a particular item of clothing is clean.

Everyone has problems from time to time. Rich or poor, we all experience challenging times. The key to happiness is in how you handle your problems. If you always think of yourself as the victim, chances are good you will always *be* the victim.

In a sermon, the preacher was talking about letting go of things that bother you. You are not supposed to worry; you are supposed to trust God. Ideally, your focus should be on God and not on your troubles. In the preacher's message, he spoke of the dangers of holding onto your troubles (causing bitterness) and, too often, drinking from that cup of toxic feelings – your personal cup of poison.

Who is this hurting? You. Whose friends are not calling because they are sick of hearing about your problems? Yours. Whose health will be affected by this? Yours. You are the only one suffering. LET IT GO. Move on with your life. Look for reasons to be happy. You can't move forward if you are living in the past.

You can't change the past but you can ruin the present by worrying over the future. ~Anonymous

2

Five Nice Things

Years ago, I was given an assignment to list five nice things I did for myself. This was at a particularly rocky point in my life, and I was quite distraught when I could not list even one nice thing I was doing for myself. I could list many nice things I did for others, but nothing for myself. As a result, my self-worth was suffering.

It is very important that you do something for yourself every day. Even if it is something as small as looking through a magazine, having an uninterrupted phone call, or reading a few chapters in a book, this seemingly simple act will keep your self-esteem in better order.

The Sick Fish Syndrome

Do you know what happens to weak/sickly fish in an aquarium? The other fish move in, slowly eating the sick fish. They dart and bite, tearing away at their victim until it finally dies.

Many of us can identify with that sick fish. Too many times, the strong "fish" in our lives move in, grabbing and taking, literally draining our energy until we're nothing but weak shells of our former selves. The strong fish can be husbands, parents, siblings, children, friends, employers – even strangers. If you keep giving, they will keep taking. And you, "the sick fish," will grow weaker and weaker. Learn to say "No." Remember, *yes* rhymes with *stress*!

Sometimes, family can drain you worst of all. If a parent is ill and you have children at home, what do you do? Do you neglect your husband and children? Do you let your teenagers go astray because you cannot be in two places at once? Do you work yourself sick trying to run two households? When you collapse from the strain, *who* is going to step in? Please take care of yourself. You are only one person. You cannot do everything; you cannot please everyone – and you need to make time for yourself each day. This is easier if you make time for God each day.

Regardless of what the demands are, YOU must be the one who says, "I just can't do it today (or this time)." It is really that simple! You are in charge of deciding the best course of action for YOU. If you broke your leg and couldn't do the things you always do for others, do you think for one minute the world would stop? Do you think the school wouldn't find a new room mom or committee member? Do you think your husband and children wouldn't find something to eat – or order out? Don't wait until you reach the end of your rope!

3

If you are living only for others, you are missing out on a great gift – You. You are important. You are blessed. You are a Child of God. When you face challenges, look to God for comfort and strength. Ask Him to help you through any sadness you are feeling. Ask Him to help you in whatever ways you need help. Ask Him to help you realize His Plan for your life – and you must be willing to make changes. *If you need to ask God into your life, see page 165.*

Energy Vampires

You have probably noticed that some people live from one crisis to the next. There was a woman who had the worst "luck" in the world. At every conversation, there was a whole new list of problems; just listening to her drained your energy. She was not interested in hearing about you, only in telling her woes. Of course, she could not understand why people avoided her. Those folks are energy vampires – they drain the life right out of you if you let them.

Another type of energy vampire comes in the form of critical people. Particularly if you are already struggling with problems, do not let others criticize you. If you cannot hang up the phone nicely, just hang up. If you are face to face and cannot make a graceful exit, just leave. You can make apologies later. Know that it is okay to say, "I don't want to talk about it." Your friend or family member should have enough respect for you to honor your wishes.

And then there are the "needy" people. You are entitled to the same respect others want from you. No one can take advantage of you unless you allow it. It might be difficult to stand up for yourself at first, and you might hurt some feelings or lose some false friends. But your needs are just as important as the other person's needs. Don't let needy people send you on a guilt trip, make you feel like the bad guy – or worse, make you do something you really don't want to do. There are actually people who have married without love because they couldn't hurt the other person's feelings. Don't let yourself be a victim.

Helping Others

Sometimes we must guard against being a control freak (parents of adult children, take note). If someone asks for your advice or help, try to help them in the kindest way possible and in the way they actually need help. Otherwise, it might be best to remain silent. Sometimes the best way to help others is to be a great listener.

When you offer advice: Some people think their way is the only way and, through insensitive remarks, they pass along their thoughts. Even if it is good advice, the "receiver" shuts down. By offering kind, constructive suggestions, both of you will feel good. Try saying, "What would you think about...?" instead of saying something that might sound sarcastic or demeaning. Sadly, many people – while trying to be helpful – have alienated their friends and children through micro-managing and unconscious criticism.

It's Not the Age, It's the Attitude

There is so much truth in that saying. We have all known folks who act old at age 40 and others who, in their 80s, are alive with energy, enthusiasm, and happiness. Don't let age stand in your way. Have you ever heard of Grandma Moses? She was born in 1860: no disposable diapers, no washer and dryer (no electricity), no car, no superstores, no central heat or A/C. Could we do it?

Grandma Moses started painting at age 75 because her arthritis became too painful to continue doing needlepoint. Her work was discovered, and she gained national attention at age 80. She was on the covers of *Time* and *Life* magazines and is probably the best known American artist in the world. Of her 1,600 paintings, some 250 were painted after her 100th birthday. (*Source: Orlando Museum of Art http://www.omart.org*)

Colonel Sanders started *Kentucky Fried Chicken* when he was 66 years old and living on monthly Social Security checks of $105 after expenses. Don't underestimate yourself. Find something that excites you. Find the passion in your life. Rediscover your joy!

I Want To Be Happy

Many people, of various ages, have a common problem: they have lost their zest for life. Some have made bad personal or financial choices; some have suffered illness for themselves, a child or a family member, or perhaps someone dear has passed. Older folks might be less able to get around. Some families have lost everything due to fire or other disasters. Or perhaps you are sad because your last child has left home and you feel like your world has come to an end. If you have lost your joy, you need to find it again. If you give it a chance, you will be surprised at your inner strength – strength you didn't even know you had!

Don't be too hard on yourself and don't expect an immediate turnaround. Give yourself some time to adjust, but be

5

thinking of how you are going to improve your life. If you have never had time for hobbies, give serious thought to things that might interest you. Go to a craft store or library for ideas. Volunteer somewhere. Find a part-time job doing something you enjoy (see ideas in Chapter 9). Join a women's group or choir at church or check a community calendar for other groups meeting in your area. Is money a problem? Many nonprofit groups don't require a financial commitment; some offer childcare at a nominal price.

A mom in her 40s volunteered to be a teacher's helper in a high school art class. She had no art experience but tried the techniques the teacher was showing the class. It turned out the mom was quite talented and even won a blue ribbon in a local contest.

If you want things to change, *you* must change them. If you want to be happy, *you* are in control of that. This quote speaks the truth: *If you always do what you've always done, you'll always get what you've always gotten.* You can choose to change things. You can choose to do things differently.

Remember that happy people may not have the best of everything, but they make the best of everything they have.

Stress Fighters

Count your blessings instead of focusing on problems. Self-pity is a waste of time and is guaranteed to make you miserable. Others do not enjoy being around people who whine and complain. Forget past mistakes and look at each day as a new chance for happiness. Each day, say "I choose to be happy." Even if problems arise, you can *still* choose to be happy as you work through a problem. Once you give up your joy, it is much harder to get it back.

Practice random acts of kindness. It makes us feel good to help others. If physical or financial help isn't a possibility, write and mail a note to someone who is feeling down, or write a note to someone who has had an impact on your life. It will mean more to them than you could ever imagine.

Laugh heartily at every opportunity. Try to avoid people who are known to criticize or complain.

Remember that everyone has challenges of some kind; it is how you deal with the challenge that matters.

Make an *Encouragement File* and put positive things in it. The file can include thank you notes you've received, complimentary emails, compliments from others (write it on a paper to include in the file), and inspirational poems or articles you find. Make a list of your good qualities and a list of your good deeds to put in the file. When you are having a bad day, go through your Encouragement File for an instant lift!

Do something nice for yourself – something you enjoy. That could include browsing leisurely in a favorite store, reading, taking a quiet walk, working on crafts or other creative activities, etc. Light a scented candle and listen to relaxing music. We all need some time alone to regenerate, to nourish our souls.

Take a mental vacation. If you are feeling stressed, remember a time that was especially pleasant. Recall your happy moments with as much detail as possible. Take deep breaths and relax.

Keep a *Blessings Journal* where you write down good things that happen; you can even include small things like "found the nail polish I had lost." On days when you feel nothing good ever happens to you, take out your journal and read it. Keeping a record of positive things will make you feel better and will help train your mind to look at life in a more positive way.

Happiness is harder to find if we are always looking for perfection and comparing ourselves with others. Don't think, "If only I had Rachel's patience, could cook like Ann, and looked like Holly." No one has *only* good qualities! We all have flaws. Concentrate on your good qualities and work to improve areas where you think there is a problem.

Don't judge others. There is no way you can know or understand everything that is going on with another person. Always be kind because people may not remember what you actually did or said, but they will always remember how you made them feel. Also, if you are always kind, you never have to worry about apologizing for something you said.

Focus on positive thoughts, that God loves you and wants you to be happy as you strive to live for Him and according to His word.

Chapter Two
'Til Death Do Us Part

And you husbands, show the same kind of love to your wife as Christ showed to the church when he died for her. (Eph. 5:25)

Marry Your Best Friend

If you are *not* married, the best advice is to marry your best friend – the person you truly enjoy spending time with, the one you can talk to for hours, who makes you laugh, lifts you up, makes you feel good about yourself. Lasting relationships are more likely when people are of similar backgrounds, are close in age, and have common interests. The following points are important:

- Pregnancy is never the right reason to marry the wrong person.
- Yes, religious differences will matter – later if not now.
- Don't rush. You might learn something later that wasn't apparent in the beginning – when we're all on our best behavior!
- If he is 15-20+ years older than you, chances are excellent you *will* become his nurse (when you are an energetic 60, he will be 75-80, possibly with major health issues).
- If there are things you don't like about this person *before* you get married, it is guaranteed you will like those things even less *after* you're married.
- If your family and friends don't like him, that's a red flag. Ask what they see in him that you don't.
- If he doesn't like your family, or you don't like his family, that will probably cause major problems as long as you are married.
- If your relationship is based primarily on sex, know that sex may always be the most important aspect of your marriage. Even if you change (things change once children come along), he will not.
- Each of you should have the other's best interest at heart. Never simply be a member of someone's fan club. He should regard you as a precious jewel, a treasure (and you should feel that way for him).
- When you have an argument, try not to confide in your mother or best friend. You will probably forgive him, but they never will.
- If he does not treat you with respect and value your opinion before you are married, he will never change.
- You and your spouse should have common interests as well as individual interests. Your life should never only be centered around his.

Respect is the Key to Success

Although we will look at various circumstances, in any relationship – husband/wife, parent/child, boss/employee – respect is the key to success. In showing respect for others, you will receive respect. Although there will always be a few jerks who try to make life miserable for others, just forgive them, forget them, and move on. Everyone has a bad day now and then, but it's difficult when you or your spouse *always* seem to have a bad day.

"I had a bad day, too!"

The best way to protect a good relationship? Don't let the problem get too big. If you are the type who keeps taking it, letting it build up inside until you finally have enough and explode – that is absolutely the wrong way to handle it. While a cooling off period may be necessary at times, don't let silence rule your house.

If your spouse walks in from work and snaps at you, what do you do? Do you snap back? Perhaps adding a personal dig?

If that's happening at your house, try this for a change: nicely say, "Gee, hon, did you have a rough day?" You *could* put your arms around him and say, "I'm sorry you had such a bad day." You should do this *even if you also had a bad day*. It's a good habit. Good things come back to you – so do bad things. If your words are not a blessing, they are not the right words.

Maybe you are a stay-at-home mom and are ready to pull out your hair after a rough day with the children. Does your husband really need to hear your frustration first? Have you picked up the house and dressed nicely to look good when he gets home? Who does he see at work? Does he work around well-dressed women? Everyone likes to feel special, and your man is no exception. Don't give other women a chance to move in; let him know he is special to you. Take time to look nice and prepare a good meal. Ask him about his day with genuine concern. Why? *Do unto others as you would have them do unto you. (Luke 6:31)*

My Husband, the Idiot?

Television today, in show after show – and in too many commercials, sets up husbands and fathers (and men in general) as idiots. Once the head of the household, the time-honored position of *Father* has too often been reduced to that of a bumbling, ineffective, uncoordinated, thoughtless, stupid dolt. Because he is so stupid, he "deserves" the abuse he gets from his quick-witted children and his "I can do everything better than you can" wife.

These shows are called comedies but, in truth, they are tragedies. They are carving away at the very core of the American family. Smart aleck remarks and snappy sarcastic comebacks are accompanied by a laugh track that appears to validate this rude, disrespectful behavior.

It is difficult to remain objective when your brain is being filled with the wrong information. It is too easy to identify with a television character; "My husband *does* act like that sometimes." Of course he does! Those shows are based on *real* human issues. Who do you think is writing them? People who have families and problems just like you! But those people are *writers* and they are being paid to create something humorous (depending upon your particular sense of humor). They don't care if it starts a fight at your house. They don't care if your children spout the same disrespectful mess to you that they heard on TV. Can your child spell r-e-s-t-r-i-c-t-i-o-n?

When one spouse stops feeling important, when it no longer seems our spouse cares what we think, that is when problems begin to grow. Make an effort to find an answer to your problem before larger problems develop. Remember that the right answer is the one that makes both people happy.

To Love, Honor and Cherish

In our wedding vows, we promise to love, honor, and cherish. One definition for "love" is *to hold dear, to cherish*. A synonym for cherish is *appreciate*. How perfect is that? You vow to appreciate him, and he vows to appreciate you!

What about honor? For marriage, the best definition is *respect and esteem shown to another*. Synonyms for *esteem* are *worth* and *value*.

Put it all together and the two of you have vowed to God that you will *hold dear, appreciate, respect,* and *give worth and value* to the other person. Think about what that means: You can't *value* your partner if you're drunk. You can't *appreciate* and *respect* your partner if you're gambling, are a shop-aholic, workaholic, or always in a bad mood. We won't even go into the adultery issue.

Basically, if you *hold dear, appreciate, respect, and give worth and value* to each other in all circumstances, the chances are excellent that you will have a long, very happy marriage.

What I Need Is A Little Respect

Respect is a funny thing. We are taught to respect our elders and those in authority. That generally works until the person does something to lose our respect.

In marriage, we begin by having and showing respect for each other. Perhaps through time, and maybe in seeing the flaws of our spouse (without regard to our *own* flaws), respect can turn to tolerance and deteriorate from there.

No one can *demand* respect. We must behave in a way that *commands* respect. If you want respect from your spouse or children, your actions must be fair, kind, and considerate. That doesn't mean you should let others walk all over you.

And here's the best part: *as ye sow, so shall ye reap (Galatians 6:7)*, meaning that whatever you plant is what you will grow. If you plant griping, criticism and discontent, guess what you will harvest? You have probably heard the saying "what goes around, comes around." That is just a variation of the "sow and reap" verse. Basically, if you *want* (to reap) respect from others, you must be willing to *give* (sow) respect first.

Sensitivity Training

There was a joke about a husband and wife at a marriage retreat. At one point, each husband was told to name his wife's favorite flower. One husband leaned over and whispered to his wife, "It's Pillsbury, isn't it?"

If your husband isn't known for his sensitivity, try taking the first step. Few people can resist kindness. When people are kind, most folks want to reciprocate in some way. If he is a little slow in responding, you might need to be a bit more direct: "It would be so nice if you would surprise me with...." (flowers, going out to eat, watching the kids for a few hours, etc.).

If you feel unappreciated, try to identify the reason behind it. It is helpful to spend time with a married couple who are kind and respectful to each other, who openly appreciate each other.

Friends can have a positive or negative impact on your marriage. If your best friend hates her husband and trashes him to you constantly, her anger and disrespect can rub off on you. It *can* affect your marriage. The same goes for your husband's friends. Especially if your marriage is a bit rocky, make sure you associate with people who speak and act in a positive way! Both of you should be sensitive to the feelings of the other.

Fighting Fair

Even in the best relationships, there will be times when you can't agree. Sometimes, it can be as simple as a mood problem or a timing problem. Sometimes the husband – or wife – just needs some time alone.

When a situation gets out of hand, one thing to remember is: *Would I talk this way to my best friend?* Your husband (and children) should be at least as important as your best friend. But emotions can run high, especially during arguments, and sometimes words are said that hurt deeply; emotionally pain can cut like a knife. Do NOT use words that hurt your partner. There are rules for arguing, just as if you were in a boxing ring.

RULES FOR ARGUING *(additional tips on page 23)*

1. Never call the other person a name. Even if you think he is lazy, you cannot say it. You CAN say, "I don't think you spend enough time working. You cannot say, "You're a lazy ____."

2. You cannot say, "You are just like your ___ (father, mother, dead-beat brother, etc.). Don't criticize the person, criticize the action.

3. No hitting – ever.

4. Do NOT say anything you might need to "take back." Once you say it, you *cannot* <u>ever</u> take it back. Don't say, "Maybe we should get a divorce," hoping it will give you the winning edge. One day, he might agree with you.

5. Keep voices as calm as possible. If one person refuses to yell, the other person will usually become more calm.

6. Don't let a fight start over something small. Sometimes the other person isn't looking for a solution to a problem as much as just wanting to talk about it. If your husband doesn't understand that, tell him plainly, "I just need to vent." Don't assume people know what you want, and don't be shy about telling them.

Fighting fair is another sign of respect for each other. You do not always have to agree completely on everything, but you should think enough of each other to always be considerate of the other person's feelings.

Whether man, woman or child, no one should ever be beaten down physically, emotionally, or spiritually. ~ Barbara Cone

Feelings Are Important

This is a counseling benefit I will share. Your feelings are important, and his feelings are important. If one of you says, "I feel like a doormat," the other cannot say, "No, you don't." You cannot criticize the way someone *feels*. Their feelings belong to them, right or wrong. If one person is angry or hurt, something has happened to make him or her feel that way.

Let's look at this example:
Spouse: "You make me so mad!!!"
You: "YOU MAKE ME MAD, TOO!" (voice is raised)
Where do you think this is going? We know it will either escalate into a big fight with lots of yelling or produce total silence.
Let's try it this way:
Spouse: "You make me so mad!!!"
You: "I'm sorry. What have I done to upset you?" That will help defuse the fight rather than give it more power.

What would happen in your house if you responded that way? Would it open a door to discussion? Consider these points:

(1) Be sincere about hearing the answer. Make sure you ask any questions needed to clearly understand the problem. It could be helpful to say, "I hear you saying…."

(2) Don't interrupt when your spouse is talking. If that is a problem, rest your hand in front of your mouth. Your spouse should make their point, then it is your turn.

(3) If you just need to vent and he is trying to fix the problem (men tend to do that), smile and say, "I just need you to listen and sympathize with me this time!" Be aware that sometimes, he needs that too.

(4) If past fights haven't been very fair, realize that both of you need to give this new method some time to work. The goal is for both of you to feel good about the outcome.

Is Divorce Really the Answer?

Does divorce seem to be the only answer? Can you afford to get a divorce? Is that going to make you happy? Is it going to make the children happy? Sometimes, the answer to that question is yes – but many times, the answer is no.

Counseling can save $$$'s: Here is an example of the *Penny Wise, Dollar Foolish* rule. "*I don't have money for marriage counseling.*" Do you know what a divorce costs? Compare a few hundred dollars, maybe more, for counseling (*pennies*) with the expense of divorce (*lots of dollars*) plus the emotional impact on you and the children. Expenses for two households, not to mention heartache and hassle for years to come = $$$'s. As a single mom, chances are good you will HAVE to work, leaving your children alone or for a daycare to raise. Not only would a strong marriage be better for all of you, but counseling is *much* cheaper than a divorce.

What will happen if you get a divorce? Along with the emotional issues, there's the never-having-enough-money issue, the working single mom issue, and much more to consider.

Let's look at it from a different perspective:

1.　　　BEFORE you get a divorce, *pretend* you are divorced. Let your husband rent a motel room for the weekend (his new home), and he takes the children. You get the weekend off. No money to rent a motel room? Of course there is. If you're getting a divorce, you must get used to wasting money. He has to live somewhere and spend money on eating, laundry, utilities, etc.

2.　　　Maybe you could send the children somewhere for the weekend while the two of you do something special. There's not enough money to go out? Is there enough money for a divorce? Go out to dinner, a movie, dancing – whatever it is that you might enjoy doing. Do whatever it takes to save your marriage. It is a lot cheaper than a divorce! Perhaps the two of you can take a weekend vacation. Call a travel agency. You might be surprised at where you can go for a small amount of money.

3.　　　Did you ever enjoy talking to each other? Make time to talk about things other than your problems. Remember better times.

4.　　　Pray – for him, for yourself, for your family, and for your marriage. Ask God to bless all of these concerns, and never ask God to change someone without asking him to change you first.

EFFORT is required to accomplish anything worthwhile. To have a good marriage, both of you must make an *effort* to work WITH the other person. This is not a "best man (or woman) wins" situation. Both of you must win.

Consider the other person's feelings. If your mother is difficult and causing problems, tell her she is hurting your marriage and she must change or stay away. If his mom is the problem, he must do the same. If you have a family member or friend living in your spare bedroom and it's driving you crazy, you and your husband must sit down and calmly decide on a date the person will leave (soon). The two of you are in this *together*. Big decisions should be made *together*. *For this cause shall a man leave his father and mother, and shall be joined unto his wife, and they two shall be one flesh. (Ephesians 5:31)*

We don't *demand* things from the person we love. We work together. Learn to say, "What do you think about....?" instead of "I want...." And remember your wedding vows: "love, honor and cherish." Each person is the giver and each person is the receiver.

The Stinker

Sometimes, you just can't come to an agreement. Even though you have done everything possible, he is still cheating or drinking or beating you and/or the children. Verbal abuse is just as real as physical abuse. In some ways, it's worse because it is so constant and, like physical abuse, will strip you of every shred of self-worth. Some folks just can't help themselves. Too often, you can't help them either. Their problems are too deep for an untrained person to reach. Sometimes they have to lose everything – their family, their job, their home and, possibly, their freedom.

If the person you married turns out to be someone you really do not know, divorce may be the only answer. You might feel comfortable seeking advice from your pastor, and try to get recommendations for a good attorney.

And It Came To Pass

No relationship runs smoothly 100% of the time. There was a lady who thought she had a perfect marriage – perfect children too. When she learned the ugly truth, she was devastated.

"How did you handle it?" I wanted to know.

"Counseling," she replied. "Counseling and my favorite Bible verse, 'And it came to pass,' because it *always* does." *This portion of a verse is found 396 times in the King James Bible, 62 times in Genesis.*

Remember that whatever is happening is temporary. How you handle a problem is important. *Learn to control your reaction to the problem.* You will find that to be much easier than trying to control the problem.

15

Chapter Three
Are Your Children a Blessing?
Bring up your child in the way he should go and when he is old, he will not depart from it. 1 Peter 3:7

Establishing Rules
RESPECT: Every household must have rules. Most important is respect. When children grow up without learning respect, it causes a lifetime of problems. *Discipline* comes from the Latin word *discipulus*, meaning pupil; to discipline means to teach. Parents are responsible for teaching their children the all-important lesson of having respect for themselves and for others. Having respect for yourself means behaving in a moral way and not making decisions that would endanger yourself or your reputation. This would include such things as dressing in a respectable manner and talking respectfully to others. Having respect for others is easier if you honestly have respect for yourself.

Tantrums – at any age – cannot be permitted. Respect is far reaching; it includes consideration for others in every circumstance. If your child starts to cry in a public place – restaurant, church, the theater (play or movie), PTA meeting, school performance, department or grocery store, etc. – you should leave. Do not expect others to listen to your crying child. From an early age, you should be teaching your child to respect you, others, and himself. Although much of this chapter is directed toward the older child, know that many bad habits are formed before the age of five. Read *Dare to Discipline* by Dr. James Dobson and *The Way They Should Go* by Laura Lou Tolles.

Do not withhold discipline from a child. Proverbs 23:13

OBEDIENCE: Even when crawling, babies should start learning the difference between good and bad choices. Toddlers, however, must learn that bad choices have strong, quick, consistent results. If you are using words like stubborn and strong-willed to describe your toddler, that child is already headed toward controlling you.

Children should respond appropriately to the word "No." This is for their safety as well as for your sanity. If little Timmy is dressed as Superman and is about to fly from the top of the stairs, you want to be able to shout "NO!" and know that he will stop. "No" should never merely be an invitation to negotiate.

If you tell your child to come and she runs the other way, don't laugh. When inappropriate behavior is rewarded by laughter, you are telling the child it is okay to behave that way. Laughter will make any problem worse. What if she thinks it will make you laugh when she runs toward a busy intersection? Hopefully, your child is learning to do what is pleasing to you. In later years, your child should understand that you always have his or her best interests at heart as you set rules and expect compliance.

YOU ARE THE BOSS: Unless your child is making the money to support your family, the home is *your* space. It is best if children can have their own space, but that space is *never* off limits to you.

Children have friends and they have parents. Parents are the boss and must always be in charge. While parents should always be loving, that is not the same as being friends. Children are not born with logic or advanced reasoning skills; those skills are developed with age. Even if you *think* your child is "6 going on 21," it really isn't true. If your children *know* you are the boss, they *expect* you to be in control. Children should show respect to their friends, their parents, and to other adults. Their friends should respect you also.

Also, remember "the boss" doesn't tell his employees about the company business. If you have serious financial or marital problems, do not confide in your children. They don't need those burdens or, worse, to feel guilt over situations they cannot control.

BEHAVING RESPONSIBLY: Parents cannot go through life with blinders on, trusting until something BIG happens. "But officer, I had no idea he would steal the car." Who are his friends? How does she spend her free time? Is she thinking about a career? Are his friends people who will always "just get by" or do they have a career plan? Ask questions, and know what is going on. Do it respectfully with love and concern, not as the parent police.

In a 1980s lawsuit, there was a woman whose son was using the McDonald's stir spoon to snort cocaine. (Before the flat plastic ones, it was a plastic stick with a tiny spoon on the end.) Honestly, I don't know how McDonalds lost that one. Where on earth was the mother? It seems *she* would be more responsible than McDonalds for her child's behavior. A rolled up dollar bill is also used to snort powdered drugs. If this mother had found her son using a rolled up dollar bill to snort his cocaine, would she have sued the United States Treasury for printing money?

When my daughter was in seventh grade, there was a classroom problem where the teacher (a coach) had thrown a chair at one of the boys. Granted, that's a little extreme, but coaches have always been a bit different from other male teachers. My daughter told me how the boy's mother had come to the school to tear the place apart. "You would do that for me, too – wouldn't you, Mom?"

"Of course I would come to the school," I said. "And my first question would be, 'What did you do to make that teacher mad enough to throw a chair at you?'" It took her a minute to understand exactly what I meant. Unfortunately, for children and teachers, too many parents are ready to defend their children – regardless of what they have done – instead of teaching the children to be responsible for their actions and respectful of others.

You cannot teach your child to be responsible if you do not accept responsibility for <u>your</u> actions. **If it is always someone else's fault, you are not accepting responsibility for your actions.**

Your goal is to raise a responsible adult, so you must encourage them to take responsibility. Showing lack of faith in their abilities/decisions will only encourage a lack of self-esteem. Look for opportunities to compliment them. Ask for their opinions. If they are routinely making bad choices, it could be a self-esteem problem, even if you have done everything possible to encourage them. It might be time to get a counselor involved.

LOVE: If love is not taught at home, they will learn about the wrong kind of love somewhere else. Your job is to love your children *while* you teach them responsibility and respect. Don't confuse love with being overly permissive. When a child becomes demanding, you are creating a monster. It will only result in future heartbreak for you and misery for your child.

As parents, one of our most important functions is to listen. Once they reach school age, it is vital that your child knows you are always interested in them. As they become teenagers, that line of communication is even more important. If you work full time, make a special time to talk to your child. If you aren't there for them, they might find the wrong people or outlet to fill that important need.

The I.Q. Test

You may have heard variations on this story, but this is what actually happened. In 1964, an experiment was conducted in a West Coast school. A research team randomly chose 20% of the students and told their teachers an I.Q. test had identified those children as exceptionally intelligent. This was not true. By the end of the year, the children had made great progress; some I.Q. scores increased by as much as 25 points. Evaluations showed these students to be superior to the other 80% of the students.

Why? Teachers enjoy working with gifted students. They treat them differently. Children, as well as adults, live up to the way they are treated. If you tell your child that he/she is stupid, worthless, a troublemaker, whatever – you are setting your child's goals. The resulting problems will affect that child for life.

If you expect the worst, you will seldom be disappointed.

Children Learn By Example

Above all, remember that children learn by example. Whether the child is two years old or 18, they are watching you. If you and your husband fight all the time, your child will think that is a normal relationship. If you never eat together as a family or have family activities, your child will learn that family time is not important. If you drive recklessly, your child will think that is normal. If you criticize and judge everything and everybody, can you guess what will be coming out of your child's mouth?

Likewise – if you dress well, your child will know the right way to dress. If you are kind to others, your child will be kind to others. If you and your spouse treat each other with respect, your child will seek people who are respectful. Whatever you do – you are teaching your children *every single day.*

Are Your Words A Blessing?

Ask your child to make a list of his/her good qualities. If they have trouble making a list, you have a problem. Your words carry a greater impact than you can even imagine. Never criticize your child. You can criticize the *action*, not the person. If you are absolutely furious beyond control, tell your child you are angry right now and will discuss it later. *Make sure you discuss it later.*

Never say, "You are such an idiot." Don't use condemning words: stupid, moron, brat – or say "You're terrible in math" (or any other subject). As you say those words, and especially if you repeat them often, you are setting the wrong goals for your child.

Look for opportunities to build your child's self-esteem. Some examples are: "Good answer!" "Thanks! I didn't think of that!" "You look nice in that outfit." "I love how you are so nice to other children." "I am so proud of you." Ask your child for their ideas and suggestions on different things.

If your child wants to do something you consider potentially dangerous or is a bad decision (like staying home alone when you don't think he is old enough to do that), instead of saying, "I said no; you're not old enough," you could say, "Because I love you so much and want to know you're safe." That way, you are telling the child your decision is based on love and not because the child is not responsible enough to be left on his own.

Treasure this time with your children. They will be adults more quickly than you can believe!

The Curse of Sarcasm

While many of us use sarcasm from time to time, it should not be the main form of communication in the home. If your family watches most television sitcoms, it will be more difficult to keep sarcasm out of your everyday conversations. Too often, sitcoms for children and teens are teaching them to be smart alecks – to their parents, teachers, friends, and siblings. While some of the comeback lines are funny when you're watching the show, they aren't so funny when your child is saying them back to you. Worse, some of the shows are teaching questionable morals.

The adult shows are even more sarcastically based. If you aren't careful, your home will resemble the sitcom as you and your husband spar verbally and include your children in these attacks.

Children begin to understand the concept of sarcasm around age 6 but do not see humor in it until age 10 or later. Even then, their straightforward thinking pattern processes sarcasm as mean-spirited. One psychiatrist writes, "*Sarcasm cuts right into a kid's self-esteem and the wounds can last a lifetime.*"

In its worst form, sarcasm is emotional abuse. Ridicule is sarcasm's evil partner. Children who live with sarcasm and ridicule on a daily basis do not grow up with good self-esteem. They must always be on guard, watching for the hidden meaning in everything that is said, and they learn to be suspicious and distrustful of others – creating lifelong problems.

Sexual Predators

While we all know this is a problem, it might be closer than you think. A 14 year old girl was molested by a janitor in her church on a Sunday morning. He approached her when she was exiting the restroom during the service – a time when few people would be wondering through the halls. Because he had gone out of his way to befriend this girl (and other girls), she was less alarmed initially – exactly what a pedophile wants. When asked why she didn't scream or fight, her response was, "I didn't want to hurt his feelings."

It is the duty of every parent to make it very clear to their children that *no one* <u>ever</u> has the right to touch them in private areas or to say inappropriate (especially sexual) things to them. Once their "friend" (whether stranger, family member, or family friend) has crossed that line, there is no room for consideration. Your children must understand that *their* feelings matter most in situations of a personal nature, and they should always tell someone they trust.

It is very important to keep an open relationship with your children and teens. Ask about people they know, and always investigate any adult relationships your child might have. Pedophiles are frequently close friends or members of the family. The standard operation is to develop a friendship with the child before sharing a "secret" – the sexual relationship. Your child should know about people like this and to immediately report inappropriate behavior.

Teen Sex

This is something you must address. One approach it is to tell your child: *You must make the choice. If you choose to risk putting an end to your freedom – to fun, going out with friends, hanging out at the mall, etc., then you can choose the risk of having a baby. (Take time to explain that, at this age, boys do not "love" girls as much as they love the idea/act of sex.) However, if you want to DO something with your life, go to college, have fun, travel, enjoy a great career, etc., you will not choose sex. You will choose boyfriends who have other interests AND have respect for you.*

Talk to your teen. Sometimes we believe we have done all the right things, but our child is still making bad decisions. If there are problems and you can't make a difference, find a counselor that shares your beliefs and values. If money is an issue, contact churches or a pregnancy center for help in finding affordable counseling.

Better Choices

It is best to do this when your children are still young, but regardless of the age, expose them to a variety of interests: music, sports, museums, theatre, horse shows, fancy restaurants, TV shows on cooking/decorating/travel, touring high priced homes – anything that will spark their creativity and interest. Your children should know there is a bigger world than school, television, and computers. Show them that great things await those who want a better life and are willing to work for it! Let them know it is important to plan ahead, to set goals and to have dreams. There is so much more to life than school, but that is all they know right now. Help them find a goal. If they don't, one day they will be old and miserable that they let their youth and time of opportunity waste away.

When There's Trouble

A popular thought is that the education system began to founder when old-fashioned discipline and values were removed from the schools. Some kids today have no respect for any level of authority (including their parents) and some, sadly, see no benefit to finishing school. These problems impact society as a whole.

Why is this happening? Sometimes it is because the parents of those children are either "allowing them to find themselves" or are too lazy to be parents and set rules. But sometimes, parents have done the right things and the child has rebelled with lying, drugs and more. Worse, what was successful parenting with one child might be totally ineffective with another child in the same family.

Any parent who says everything is perfect at their house is less than truthful. Even the best kids can pose challenges. However, there are varying degrees of problems. If your child needs strange hair colors and numerous facial piercings to "find" themselves, they are lost – and you might be too. The truth? Being "unique" won't do anything but make people stare and wonder. More visible unique markings (large tattoos, lip/tongue piercings, etc.) may keep them from <u>ever</u> getting a decent job (one they actually enjoy). Being *too* unique is usually a major cry for help.

The following section addresses establishing a better relationship with your child. If the problems are deeper, and especially if your child is having problems with cutting or other issues that indicate lack of self-worth, he/she needs to talk with someone other than you. You should consider a Christian counselor.

If your church isn't staffed for counseling, call a pregnancy center or women's shelter for help. Some centers have counselors or can refer you to other sources. You must always meet with the counselor first or in a combined session with your child to be sure the counselor will best suit the needs of your particular situation.

Do You Want To Fix the Problem?

To develop a better relationship with your child, these tips may work. *(Some of these points are also helpful for marital discussions.)* Accept that you will do whatever you can to improve the situation. Make a list of specific issues you want to address, then….

- Set up a time to talk. No cell phones or other interruptions are allowed (for either of you). No siblings allowed. Leave the house if necessary. Neutral territory might be best – maybe the park or a restaurant during non-peak hours.

- Regardless of what has happened, begin by saying something kind or complimentary to your child. Remember the goal is for both of you to feel good about the outcome.

- Ask what is going on (not "Why did you do that?") and LISTEN to what he/she has to say. "I don't know" is not an answer. Some silence is okay, but encourage your child to talk. You can say, "Have I done something to upset you?" You cannot say, "Haven't I given you enough/done enough for you?" No guilt trips allowed.

- Be open to the fact that the problem might be you, but keep in mind that you are trying to raise a responsible adult. They must learn to take responsibility for their decisions. Fight the impulse to jump in and defend yourself or any action. Just listen until it is your turn to talk.

- Stay calm and answer ONLY when you have given yourself time to digest what is said. Answer only when you know you can say something in a positive way.

- You absolutely cannot ask any trick questions – the ones where your response is "Aha!" Not only should you not ask those types of questions now, you should *never* ask them.

- Do not raise your voice and do not criticize. Criticism will shut down the conversation. Just listen and ask questions.

- Do not be afraid to apologize to your child. Apologizing does not mean admitting guilt or weakness. You can say, "I am so sorry you feel that way" and *mean it.* Then, you can follow with, "How can I help? What can we change?"

- Is there a positive role model your child admires? (an adult family member, friend or teacher who has made an impact on your child, not a celebrity/sports/music figure) Ask your child to think about his/her previous choices and if those choices might be a source of future pride – if those stories are the ones he wants to tell *his* children. Ask if he would want his child to someday make those same choices.

- If your child is cutting herself (check wrists, legs), ask if she might be thinking of someday wearing a beautiful prom dress or wedding gown. Has she thought about how she might look in five years? (Many kids only think a few days ahead.) Does she want to explain scars to her future children? Does she want to marry someone who cuts (meaning he has problems too)? Cutting can be a very serious emotional problem and may require professional counseling. (See more below.)

- Many kids haven't thought about the future. Is there a plan for college? Technical school? An interest in a particular field? Can you, as the parent, help them find a direction? Establish a goal? Identify something they enjoy or a skill that could be a career?

- Future employers will be looking for people with a positive attitude who are helpful and who work well with others.

- *Remember, every good lesson must end on a positive note.*

The "troubled teens" of today have more in common than wearing black clothes and heavy black makeup. Two main subcultures are *Goth* and *Emo*. Google *goth vs emo* on the Internet for more info. With Emo kids, watch for cutting; wrist bands are often worn to cover cut marks. Watch for long sleeves, hoodies, and long pants worn during hot weather. Watch for depression and movies/music with depressing themes, and watch for expressions of anger. This type problem involves self-worth issues and, even if you are a counselor, your child needs to talk to someone other than you.

Just like adults, children are looking for a place to belong. Regardless of your relationship, kids need the acceptance of other kids. They need friends – friends with similar (positive) interests.

The kids who stay out of trouble generally have a sense of belonging. For some, it is sports. They *belong* to the football/baseball/basketball team, cheerleading squad, dance team, and so on. Some find their spot in the school band or in clubs (not gangs). Most schools offer a number of different clubs. Or what about church? Does your church offer a good youth group? Teens need to feel good about what they are doing and be accepted by their peers. They need friends with similar interests and, hopefully, friends and adults who will lead them in a positive direction.

If your child cannot find his/her place within the school or church, or if you don't have the financial resources for your child to participate in other activities (or a way to get the child home after a club activity), perhaps there is something outside of school that would be interesting. Music lessons, community theatre or choir are often good choices. What about a 4-H group, volunteering at an animal hospital or shelter, or maybe with a company that trains dogs to help disabled people? For many kids (and adults), they want to do something that *matters*. They want to make a difference. Sometimes they don't know it – and that's where you come in: to teach, to lead, to help them find their way. When the kids don't *belong* somewhere, when there is no sense of purpose, they tend to drift toward others who are also drifting.

Above all, your child needs to know you love them. Regardless of the problem (or your sadness over what the child has done), you cannot move forward until you reach a point where you can have a normal conversation with your child – meaning you can laugh, joke, and talk about things other than the problem. You can do this even though the child is on full restriction/grounded.

Lead, Follow, or Get Out of the Way

When children (especially young teens) first realize you are only a human being and not perfect, it is a crushing blow to them. As they recover from that reality, they begin testing to see who is really smarter, to see if you should really be in charge.

As a "horse person," this comparison was most interesting. When horses are in a herd, there is one leader, the alpha male. In the wild, the alpha male is the stallion (stud). In domestic herds, the alpha is the strongest male horse. Daily, other horses challenge to see if he is showing signs of weakness. If the alpha can't defend his position, he loses his spot and must fight to regain it. The fight is physical – kicking and biting. In the wild, they will fight until one dies or leaves the herd.

Let's compare that with problems of today:
1. The young stud challenges the alpha male (could be dad or mom). *Johnny comes home with bright blue spiked hair and a ring in his eyebrow.*
2. The alpha backs off. "He's just going through a phase. We'll ignore it and let it run its course." *Your lack of action is seen as weakness.*

3.   Johnny now assumes alpha position. *Drugs, comes and goes as he pleases, more piercings. You might as well not even live there.*
4.   The "old alpha" (you) either hangs his head in defeat or decides to try to regain the position of authority. *It's harder to regain the throne than to stay in power; ask any deposed dictator. It's going to be a fight; be prepared for emotional bloodshed.*

This problem is not a male-only field. Your young filly can take over just as quickly. Decide who is going to be in charge, then act accordingly. If you are the leader of your family, you must set rules, set goals, set punishments – and follow through.

Please realize you must choose your battles. Nothing is gained by fighting constantly over every little thing. While big issues must be addressed immediately and with authority, conflicts can be resolved only if both you and your child are willing to give on some things and to always show respect for each other.

The Fifth Commandment

Honor your father and your mother, so that you may live long in the land the Lord your God is giving you (Exodus 20:12). Many have questioned how God could command honor for a parent who has done nothing to deserve honor. What about parents who ridicule, humiliate or abuse their children? Do these parents deserve honor?

Honor does not mean merely doing everything someone says, nor does it mean to show undeserved respect. Many scholars believe this commandment literally means "bring honor to." We bring honor to our parents by living a respectable life, by making good choices. Parents are responsible for teaching their children about honor and respect. If children are taught to honor and respect God, it is easier to teach those children to honor and respect God-loving parents.

As we all know, raising children is the one thing that should come with an instruction book. We can do damage without even realizing it. Actually, there *IS* an instruction book, **The Holy Bible**. The Ten Commandments *(Exodus 20)* are a great place to start. All ten are important, but it is really all about respect: respect God, respect your spouse, and respect others. If every parent could teach their children the true meaning of respect, it would change the world.

Chapter Four
Penny Wise, Dollar Foolish
Blessings on all who reverence and trust the Lord – on all who obey him! Their reward shall be prosperity and happiness. Psalm 128:1-2

This is not your traditional "how to become rich by saving money" advice. These suggestions are not for those who don't know where to invest the $500,000 Uncle Joe left them. This is for the many people who need to know it is okay to start small.

Saving money is something many of us have trouble doing. So many times, we put money aside but need it far too quickly. Many families are one paycheck away from losing everything. If the husband or wife suddenly lost their job, there would be nothing to fall back on. You probably know people like this – families who lost their homes when seemingly secure jobs disappeared. There was no savings account and another job didn't come through soon enough.

Aside from knowing that you're supposed to be saving for your retirement, did you know you should have enough money in the bank to pay *at least one month* of bills? That means mortgage/rent, car payment(s), utilities, charge card payments, and whatever else you owe. Don't forget about groceries, gas for the car, car insurance, medicine, and more. Hopefully, by being conscientious and working hard to put money aside, you can save enough to carry you through three months of bills. Having nothing to fall back on is how you get behind. And once you get behind, it is very hard to catch up – but not impossible! Remember that everyone goes through challenging times. Change is not always a bad thing.

If you do not have a regular savings account, you need to work on that. If you *do* have a savings account and are able to contribute regularly, good for you! Regular contributions are important – and even small amounts add up to make a difference.

Having No Money Is Depressing

Have you ever sat with your head in your hands, praying with all your heart, wondering when – or how – things were going to improve? If not, you are indeed blessed. Knowing you are totally out of money gives you a low feeling like nothing else can. It is a most humbling experience.

Having no money changes people. You actually think about bank robbers and thieves in a different light. You *can* become desperate. There is fighting in the home. Your children feel the tension. They worry and fuss; maybe they cry more often. Ask any school teacher. Whatever problems the adults are having affects the children every day. *(Please try not to involve your children in money or personal matters.)*

Many years ago when our town was still small, there was a young mother (late teens) who reached a point of total desperation. She put her new baby in a car seat and drove to the bank. At the drive-through, she sent her robbery note through the tube. Of course, the bank called the police, who immediately appeared and took the girl away. Her decision – her desperation – changed her life.

Although her experience would now be one of the "stupid criminals" stories, I couldn't help feeling so very bad for this girl. She had obviously considered all of her options, and she saw no other way out.

Churches are often the first place people go when they need help. Spiritual help, of course, is greatly needed in stressful times, but churches can help in other ways. Some have food banks; some will give small amounts of cash; some have clothes closets; some might even be able to help with employment – or direction. *Ye have not because ye ask not. (James 4:2)* Ask, and be willing to make changes in your life. Remember that the Lord is faithful to those who are faithful to Him, and that He always knows your heart. Know, too, that the church is not there to support your family – only to lend a helping hand.

Because we are self-employed, we know things can be tough. If you are self-employed and haven't been able to put enough money aside, you *know* your finances are going to be tight if there is no work coming in. There is always the possibility of an unexpected dry spell, a long gap between jobs when there is *no* paycheck coming – you are in it alone. There is no unemployment check. You will not have *any more money* until you get another job.

When money is tight, there are ways to cut back. You might buy cheaper cuts of meat, get creative with ground beef or look for healthy no-meat meals. *(See pages 105-106 for vegetable and bean meals.)* Instead of reaching for paper towels, use cloth ones that can be washed. Clip coupons – but only for exactly what you need. In most cases, store brands taste just fine. Plan your week's menu around what is on sale at the grocery store. When meat is on sale, stock up so you never end up paying full price. Always shop with a list to eliminate buying on impulse. Buy a box of healthy snack bars and keep some with you so you are not tempted to stop at a convenience store when you get hungry at work or while running errands. And try not to use charge cards for routine purchases.

Do not let money woes ruin your marriage. Remember, you are a team. You are in this together. Don't accuse your partner if at all possible. Unless he gambled or drank up every cent you had, place the blame elsewhere. If careless shopping is the culprit, shame on you. Wait for things to go on sale or do without unnecessary items.

Sometimes things happen; we cannot know what tomorrow might bring. If you are married, the two of you should discuss possible solutions. Make a plan. Keep your team intact. Promise each other that – somehow – you will put money aside, that you will have a savings account, that *next time* you will be prepared. In the next chapter, we will look at some creative ways to save.

Such a Dilemma

We work at saving every day. We don't struggle with which bank offers the best interest rate on CDs because our CDs are the ones that play music. I used to listen to a radio talk show where people called in about money matters. Too many times, the story was along this line: "I'm 45 years old; my house is paid off; my cars are paid off; I have no credit card debt and was wondering how to invest this $200,000 that's left over." What a dilemma! Many of us would love to have that particular problem! I finally stopped listening to the show because the investment and vacation questions left me depressed.

Don't forget that rich folks have money problems too, just on a different scale. "Carla" worked for a collections company and was making her usual "how much money can you send" calls. For one customer, Carla patiently waited while the lady explained their financial woes. "We had to let our *gardener* go," the woman wailed. Oh my, such a dilemma.

And then there are the folks who brag by complaining: "Can you believe I paid $200 for these slacks? Just to get this particular shade of eggplant!" Oh, please!

We are going to talk more about ways that can save you money – even when you don't seem to have an extra penny *ever!* This is not advice from the rich to the poor – it is from one friend to another. It is for regular, everyday people who need help making it from month to month – or week to week.

You don't want to get so dragged down in details that you don't know where to start. Hopefully, this helpful, to-the-point advice will make a difference in your life.

Penny Wise, Dollar Foolish

Penny wise, dollar foolish is an old phrase. If you have not heard it, an example might be that you drive five miles away because gas is five cents a gallon cheaper at the X station. Let's say your tank holds 20 gallons and your car will go 20 miles on one gallon. If you drive to the X station and buy 20 gallons of gas, you will save $1 (20 gallons x 5¢ = $1). By driving five miles there and five miles back, you put ten extra miles on your car and used a half gallon of gas to save a grand total of one dollar. In reality, you didn't save anything.

Maybe a distant grocery store has a deal on something you want. You are going to that store for only one item. A nearby store has the same item, but you can save $3 by going to the distant store. Wise choice? No. The time and gas it takes to get there (plus the wear and tear on your car) means you actually spent *more* money. To save *pennies*, you spent *dollars*.

Grocery stores (and other stores) offer "deals" on *Loss Leaders*. This means they are advertising a sale price on an item they are selling [1] at a very small profit, [2] at no profit (their cost) or [3] at less than what they paid for it.

Loss Leaders are designed to get you into the store. Studies have shown that once you are inside, you most likely will buy other things – probably a number of items. *Beware of extra warranties and insurance on electronics and other things.* That is how they can offer cheap prices on a few items – because they make their profit on the other things you buy and on accessory items!

What about money-saving coupons? Coupons are designed to get you to try new products (translation: spend more money). After all, you are *saving* 50¢ or perhaps $1 to try a new product. However, if you are buying something you really don't need, you are not saving money.

Coupons save money if you use them <u>only</u> for what you *need*. For baby products, especially diapers, coupons can be great. If you are a coupon shopper, go to **www.couponmom.com** and sign up (free) for great info and lots of coupons.

Save money and stress on laundry day. See Chapter 13.

Five Truths

We all know how important it is to *save* because you never know when something is going to come along to *take* it. If you save everywhere you can, you will be able to splurge occasionally. Also, you know there are always unexpected expenses.

I used to get so upset when unexpected expenses came along. Each time we had a little extra money, it seemed we had a major repair due on the house or car. The timing was enough to drive a person mad. It always came down to, "Guess there's no vacation again *this* year."

For most of us, life can be condensed to these five truths:
- God is always in control.
- Death will come to all of us.
- There are always people who are worse off than you are.
- A major medical expense or major repair (car or house) will come along, usually when you can least afford it.
- At some point, things will change – this is true even when everything is going well and you are happy!

Accepting these five truths has helped me deal with the unexpected. I know I am not the only person who has problems. I know there are many people with problems much worse than mine. And I know that the only way to deal with a problem is to pray about it and meet it head on. Don't waste time finding someone or something to blame. Don't get mired in the "what if" possibilities. Take responsibility for <u>your</u> problem and find a solution.

Working Full Time vs. Full Time Mom
Can you save money and stay at home with your children?

Should you get a full time job or should you be a full time mom? Has this been a dilemma for you? Do you work, work, work and have virtually nothing to show for it by the time you pay for childcare and other work-related expenses? Moms work for different reasons. Some work because their income makes a big difference in the family. Perhaps they are the primary wage earner. Some moms work so their family will have health insurance. But what about moms who are working basically to keep their children in childcare?

If you are trying to make that decision, please consider the following:

(1) If you have the financial option, your children are better off with you than being raised by strangers (or other family), and

(2) Perhaps you can supplement your income from home. (See Chapters 8 & 9)

If you are struggling to decide whether you should work full time or be a full time mom, make a list with two columns.

In *Column One*, write your salary minus income taxes. (Taxes are about 15% of your salary.)

In *Column Two*, estimate the cost of child care, the salary you will lose when you are home with your sick child, clothing you need for the workplace, gasoline, lunch and snacks, maintenance for your car (repairs and tires), personal needs (haircuts, makeup, etc.), lunches you buy on the days you can't take something from home, and so on. Health insurance is a consideration.

Total *Column Two* and subtract that amount from the *Column One* total. How much money is left? Is it actually *costing* you money to work? Are the totals close enough to where you can justify staying home with your child/children? Could you do something part-time from home that would equal or be greater than what is left after paying childcare and working expenses?

How does your husband feel about you being a full time mom? If *his* mother always worked, he might not be as open to you being a full time/stay-at-home mom. The two of you must sit down and talk seriously about the future of your children.

Look at examples of families around you. Overall, the children who get into the most trouble and have the most problems are the ones whose parents both work full time. Children with too much free time will crave attention, and they may fill that need through the computer, negative peer pressure, gangs, or other problem areas.

If you can be a full time mom, that is the best choice to make for your children. If your situation does not allow that, there is no need for guilt; we all do the best we can. Just be there for your children in every way possible.

Chapter Five
Save Your Money
Dishonest money dwindles away, but he who gathers money little by little makes it grow. Proverbs 13:11

Since money is such an issue for so many, we will look at different ways to save money. *BUT I DON'T HAVE ANY MONEY TO SAVE!* I have said those same words – more than once. I promise you the following methods will work. You will learn to save money. We are not talking about thousands of dollars; however, persistence – over time – will have you well on your way.

Let's take a look at where your money goes. Make a list of your monthly bills: rent/mortgage payments, car payments, charge cards, utilities (electric, gas, water, trash pick-up, phone), and groceries. Don't forget gas for the car, car insurance, health insurance, homeowner/renter's insurance, etc. That is the amount required to run your household, your basic necessities.

Now – consider clothing and shoes for your family. If you don't have a teenager yet, just wait! I don't know about teenage boys, but girls are expensive – even without designer labels.

There are doctor and dentist bills, vet bills, car repairs, and new tires. There are family gifts: birthdays, graduations, weddings, new babies, and the expense of Christmas holidays. It's a bit overwhelming to see it all in writing. But you must be realistic, especially if you tend to splurge on items that might be unnecessary.

Savings Plan A
You might have heard you should always "pay yourself first." That means you put *some* money (10% or more) in the bank from every paycheck you get. The philosophy here is to put the money into your savings account *before* putting it into your checking account or, even worse, into your wallet. If you never have it, you won't miss it. If you learn to live without that $10, $20, $50 or more, you will have a good start on your savings account.

The Envelope, Please
If you don't have a savings account, here is a great way to start: put an envelope in a drawer or in a shoebox in your closet. Unless you and your husband can do this as a team, hide it where NO ONE will find it – kids or husband – and *don't tell them about it.*

Put a $1 bill (or more) in the envelope. Think about trips to fast food restaurants, convenience stores, grocery stores, etc. For goodness sake, a large pack of gum costs more than a dollar! If you can, put at least one dollar in the envelope each day, at least a few dollars a week. If you have the *it's just a dollar* attitude toward spending money, it will be harder to save money. Don't spend *just a dollar* on fast food, coffee, snacks, etc., unless you can put the same amount in your savings envelope.

Try keeping a list of every penny you spend for one month and how you spent it. You will be very surprised to see the total.

If you chew a lot of gum, instead of buying packs that cost $1+ (package of 15 sticks), buy the big bag of eight packs with five sticks each. They generally cost around $2-$2.50 and you get 40 sticks. Watch for sales. Chew half sticks to stretch it further.

Watch your savings grow. When you have enough to open a savings account, do it! It is too easy to borrow from your envelope if a large amount of money is at home. Keep saving your dollars, and keep adding to your savings account. Get free deposit slips from the bank.

Try not to take money from this account. Emergencies will arise, but try to find other ways to deal with them. Do not think about your savings as the first answer to a money problem. Once you deplete the account, you will have to start over again with one dollar in the envelope. You don't want to get discouraged!

If your checking account is at the same bank as your savings, link the accounts together so the bank will take money from your savings if your checking account runs short. Banks charge a lot of money for bounced checks (NSF/insufficient funds). Your savings account could save you money if you make a mistake in your paperwork. Almost everyone has messed up a checkbook at some point! If you use a debit card, write every debit in a check register book (free from your bank), keep your balance current, and check your account often (daily if necessary).

If you borrow from your savings account, repay it quickly. And watch out for other bank fees. Fees can eat up your savings if money is frequently withdrawn from that account.

How many envelopes do you need?

Do you have a job where you are only paid once a month? Even if you are paid more often, are you out of money at the end of the month? This system might work for you:

Buy a small box of envelopes. On payday, cash your check and go home prepared to set up your envelopes – right then. Make an envelope for your rent or mortgage payment and one for each monthly bill: utilities, charge cards, etc. Make one for savings and make four envelopes (for four weeks) for each category: groceries, gas, etc. Remember some months have five weeks! Don't forget quarterly payments (like insurance); add to it each month. Keep a "miscellaneous" envelope for car repairs, tires, etc. Have an envelope for medical expenses. Re-use the same envelopes each month. Don't forget a "fun" envelope so you can splurge on occasion. If you are keeping a savings envelope, put it in a different place so you will not be tempted to use that money.

DO NOT tell anyone about your "banking" system – not your children, not your friends. No one should know you have an amount of cash in your home. Although you might trust your best friend, she might mention it to someone who isn't quite as honest. And children – bless their hearts – I can hear it now: *"Wow! You should see all the money MY mom has, right in the top drawer!"* Keep your money a secret. You don't need other problems.

Savings Plan B

Plan B is saving on a smaller scale, but it is better to have a little than to have nothing. Get a clear, quart-sized jar (like a mayonnaise or canning jar). If it needs to be secret, hide it. If you are saving for a new washing machine, swing set or vacation, it's fun to leave the jar out and make it a family project.

Only put quarters in this jar. Every time you get a quarter, find one under the sofa cushion, in the washing machine, etc., put the quarter in your jar. You can watch your money growing! When the jar is full, you should have about $100. Get free coin wrappers from your bank, wrap all your quarters, then start filling your jar again.

Some banks and stores offer a coin-wrapping service for a fee. Don't give them your money – do it yourself. Get coin wrappers (buy them only if you must) and count your coins at home. When the coins are wrapped, take them to the bank for paper money and start working on filling your jar again.

Other Money-Saving Tips

Tip #1: When you go to the grocery store, get an extra $5 or $10 (or more) cash, and put that extra money in your savings account. You cannot cheat – the extra money MUST go into the savings account.

Tip #2:   Pretend your savings account is a monthly bill and "pay" that bill every month.

Tip #3:   If you have a checking account but too often run short and bounce checks, take some of your newly saved money and deposit it in your checking account – but *do not include it in the balance.* In your checkbook register, put a note to yourself that the money is not included in the balance (so you can balance your account later). That way, if you *do* get down to a $5 balance, you might avoid having a bounced check because of your "hidden" money.

Tip #4:   Keep a "spare change" jar. In this jar, put in all coins <u>except</u> quarters (you already have a jar for quarters only). Do not spend *any* coins. Each night, take the change out of your wallet and put all of it in the jar. Don't count your money until the jar is full. You will see a greater profit if you do not include pennies! Use coin wrappers like you do for your jar of quarters.

Tip #5:   Have a yard sale, but put profits into your savings account. Or put half of the profits into your account. Keep your focus on saving money. To increase profits, see *Yard Sale Tips* in Appendix.

And speaking of yard sales – if you love GOING to them but cannot control your spending or find that you come home with things you're not even sure you will ever use – STOP GOING. Or, only take $20 with you. When your money is gone, go home. If *your* yard sale consists mainly of things you have bought at *other* yard sales, you are out of control!

Tip #6:   Some newspapers run free classified ads for personal items. If you don't have enough items for a garage sale, you might want to advertise some of the higher-priced items. Or if you have larger items, especially furniture or large children's toys, you can usually sell those things for more money in the newspaper than you could at a yard sale. Look around for "deals."

Check out **www.craigslist.org**. This website is a great, free place to advertise items for sale. It also has a FREE category, where people are giving away items, and you can place a free "wanted" ad if you are looking for something specific. Please be very cautious anytime you are dealing with strangers. **www.Freecycle.com** is another great place to get free items. No money ever changes hands. You can give <u>and</u> receive!

Tip #7: Consignment shops are an option for selling clothing, but make sure you get all the facts. Remember those stores are in business to make money. Baby and toddler clothes generally sell best.

Tip #8: If you smoke, think seriously about quitting. Smoking is bad for you *and* expensive. See page 44 for lots of tips.

~~~~~~~~~~~~*~~~~~~*

Tithing

On a personal note, let's talk about tithing. If you don't belong to a church, you might be missing out on one of the greatest joys of life. If your church is *not* providing peace, joy and comfort, visit other churches. If you *are* going to church, are you tithing?

Your tithe should be ten percent of your income. It must be given out of love and never begrudgingly. God has given you the ability to make money, and you are thanking Him – and expressing your faith that He will provide for you – by giving ten percent of your earnings. If you give willingly to God, He will bless you in ways you can't even imagine.

There was a time when our finances were in a big mess. It took five years to pay off the doctor bills when our second child was born. Our minister said, "If you can't tithe, God understands. Don't worry about it and start tithing when you can. Your work in the church can be your tithe. There were years when I couldn't tithe, and it's okay." *(At the time, I didn't know his life hadn't been so great either.)*

I took his advice and became very active in the church. Our financial situation grew worse. We were close to losing everything when I heard a radio sermon on tithing. I prayed and put money in the plate that Sunday. By Wednesday, money started coming in. My self-employed husband was getting jobs. It would take time, but we could see a difference. More important, we now had hope.

"Tithing is your gift to God. Working in the church is your sacrifice to God." ~ *Anonymous*

"Bring the whole tithe into the storehouse, that there may be food in my house. Test me in this," says the Lord Almighty, "and see if I will not throw open the floodgates of heaven and pour out so much blessing that you will not have room enough for it."
Malachi 3:10

Chapter Six
Spending Money, Gift Giving Ideas, Thank You Notes & Party Etiquette
He who pursues righteousness and love finds life,
prosperity and honor. Proverbs 21:21

What is a Splurge?

Technically, a *splurge* is something you really don't need. However, YOU are the only one who can determine whether or not you need something. Sometimes, the need might be emotional – and you must be careful about spending money if you are feeling depressed. It's like the other unwritten law: *don't go grocery shopping when you're hungry* (because you end up buying things you really don't need).

If you are on an emotional shopping spree, try to window shop – don't buy. Promise yourself to splurge ONLY on one candy bar, coffee drink, etc. You will be proud of yourself for resisting temptation, and you won't be depressed with the things you bought trying to make yourself feel better – or when the credit card bill arrives.

Justifying a Splurge

Most of us will justify splurging on occasion. Even when money is tight, sometimes we simply *must* buy something! It just doesn't seem fair that we work every day and can't spend any money on ourselves. Self-sacrifice is different for each person. Don't deprive yourself until you go on a spending binge. Rather than buying a lot of small things, save toward something big – so you know you will have a reward for your sacrifice. Remember that lots of small purchases add up to big amounts.

Credit Card Logic

The best rule is: *Don't buy it if you cannot afford to pay cash.* The pay-later plan introduced by credit/charge cards has ruined the credit rating of many people and, for some, it has ruined their lives financially. Credit cards (as we know them today) began in 1966. Do you know what people did before credit cards? They *saved their money* until they had enough to buy the item they wanted.

Today, people go berserk because their food at McDonald's takes longer to prepare than they think it should. No one wants to wait for *anything.* No one wants to take the time to save for a new TV, computer, etc. when they can get it today on credit. And who would have thought fast food restaurants would accept credit cards? If you cannot afford to eat out, DO NOT put it on a credit card.

Before splurging on an item, consider your monthly interest fee. If you buy something on sale and are paying $30 ($60 or $80+) in interest each month, the interest fee will likely cancel out any money you were trying to save.

Buying Gifts

Please don't buy gifts you can't afford to give. You should give from the heart (a nice card with a lovely message inside is always appreciated) and not just a brand name that "says" you spent a lot of money. Do not buy gifts that must be displayed unless you KNOW the receiver will like it. And don't ruin your budget trying to buy fancy gifts for others. What about a Gift Basket?

The Gift Basket

Gift baskets are designed specifically for the individual, are always appreciated, and save you money. They are wonderful for everyone: men, women, teens, and children. Buy baskets on sale or at garage sales or thrift stores. Keep a supply of curling ribbon and tissue paper (bought on sale, of course). At any time, you can make a wonderful, thoughtful gift.

In the basket, put in a few sheets of tissue paper (white or colors); arrange your items in a decorative way, and stream curling ribbon from the handle. Use enough ribbon – long strands – to make it more festive. The following suggestions are mostly from a budget-friendly view. Some ideas are:

- **Movie Basket:** Buy a gift certificate (the price of renting one movie) from a local movie rental store, add a two liter soft drink (or the person's favorite drink), bag(s) of microwave popcorn, and a couple of candy bars. *Great gift for a guy friend when you don't know what else to give him!*

- **Garden Basket:** Include a spade or other garden tools, potted plant(s) or nice seeds, and a pair of gloves (price can range from $1 to $15). A straw hat or visor tied onto the handle is a cute touch. Just look around the garden area of your favorite store for great ideas.

This basket can be beautiful for a small amount of money, or you can spend lots of money on fancy plants and gardening items!

- **Child's Basket:** The *garden basket* is excellent if the child likes to play in the dirt (and most do). Include a spade, child-sized gloves, and a few easy-to-grow plants or seeds (marigolds, impatiens, petunias, etc.).

  Or make a *fun basket* with some dollar store items: bubbles, sidewalk chalk, some toys or hair accessories, a coloring book and crayons for younger children. Add a juice box or a couple of packs of Kool-Aid and lollipops or gum. Most children prefer quantity over quality!

  Caution: make sure you get things that will work; some dollar store items are not designed to last very long!

- **Teen Basket:** Movie basket or car care bucket works for guys. Girls love scented sprays and lotions, bath items, candles, jewelry, picture frames, key chains, candies, etc.

- **Car Care Bucket:** Buy an inexpensive bucket instead of a basket. You can go cheap or spend big bucks. Choose from: sponge, hose nozzle, tire cleaner, car soap, wax, drying cloth, interior cleaner, roll of good quality paper towels, etc.

- **Fruit Basket:** Traditional but always appreciated. Take the basket with you to the grocery store. Pre-made fruit baskets generally have shredded paper in the bottom of the basket. This is called filler; it fills space (in larger baskets), gives air to the fruit, and prevents bruising. Take basket *with some tissue paper for filler* in it to the store, then choose the fruit. Depending on the basket size, select a grapefruit or two plus any or all of: oranges, red and green apples, plums, pears, etc. Top the basket with a few bananas or a small bunch of grapes.

  OR make a "mini" basket of red and green grapes – or a basket of strawberries. A small box of special cookies or candies could also be included. A Mini Basket is a perfect thank you or hostess gift.

- **Tea (or Coffee) Basket:** If you know the person loves tea, buy a box of specialty tea from the grocery store and add a pretty package of cookies. Sprinkle in a few hard candies, peppermints, or chocolates. For larger baskets, add more teas and cookies. A pretty mug is also a nice touch.

- **Wine Basket:** Buy a good bottle of wine and some fancy cookies or candies. You could also make an Anniversary Basket: a bottle of champagne (or sparkling/non-alcoholic) and two champagne flutes with some other goodies.

- **House Warming Basket:** Give cleansers, sponges, paper towels, etc. For a bridal or baby shower, you could use a small clothes basket (plastic or wicker) to fill with goodies.

- **Pet Lover Basket:** Make a pet basket for your animal-loving friends. Include a grooming brush, cat or dog toys, a magazine for dog or cat lovers, and treats.

- **Horse Lover Basket:** Put together a basket for your favorite horse lover. A bag of horse treats, grooming brush, horse magazine, and hoof glitter are ideas. Add a colorful bunch of carrots with green tops or a few apples!

- **Goody Basket:** If you're stuck for an idea, make a basket of different types of candies, snack items, fancy cookies, or homemade goodies. See examples are:

  - **Snack Basket:** include nuts, crackers, cheese(s), summer sausage, etc.

  - **Thinking of You Basket:** small basket of fresh strawberries and blueberries. Some loose candies are always a nice touch.

  - **Strawberry Shortcake Basket:** slices of pound cake or Angel Food cake, strawberries, and whipped cream.

Be creative. You can make **cooking** or **sewing** baskets, **get well baskets** (magazines, candles, lotions, plus something to do – crossword puzzle books, puzzles, etc.) – the list is endless!

Homemade Coupons

What about homemade coupons for services? You can give a coupon for a home-cooked meal, house cleaning, babysitting, car wash, lawn care, etc. Homemade coupons are great ideas for adults or children who want to give something but don't have any money! It is also a fun gift to give adult friends or family, and all it costs is your time.

For those who can create on the computer, that's great. However, you can also make your own with a pen and ruler.

This is a wonderful way for a child to give a meaningful gift without spending any money. Your child could use crayons or markers to make coupons like "Good for one kitchen clean up." As a bonus, you will be teaching your child the benefits of making time for others!

What About Thank You Notes?

Many consider thank you notes to be a nuisance, but have you ever sent a gift and never heard anything? Was it received? Was it even delivered? You don't know. Did the recipient like it? Was it appreciated? Aaah – that's the bottom line. Perhaps the person DID appreciate it – but not enough to let you know.

Question: When should you send a thank you note?

Answer: Whenever you receive a gift. It is also entirely permissible to "double thank" – in person or by phone, followed by a note. Grandparents should be thanked. Some grandparents are constantly giving gifts, so an occasional note along the lines of *thanks so much for the many things you do* would be nice.

It is appropriate to send a thank you note following a party.

If you receive a birthday or congratulatory card (even without money in it) or a get well card, you should call the sender and thank them for thinking of you.

Even if you do not like the gift you received, you still owe a note. Try to send your note within a week after receiving a gift; however, "better late than never" applies. If you owe a note, start writing! *(Sample thank you notes on page 182.)*

Party Etiquette

(1) When issuing party invitations, send them at least two weeks before the event; 3-4 weeks before for busy holiday or Christmas parties, and 6 weeks before a wedding.

(2) Always respond to an R.S.V.P., preferably when you receive the invitation but certainly by the date given (or three days before the party). The hostess needs to know how many people are attending so correct amounts of food, paper goods, party favors, etc. can be purchased.

(3) Arrive either at the designated time or within ten minutes after the start of the party. Inform your hostess if you will be late or if you need to arrive early. Never be the last one to leave unless you are invited for an extended visit.

(4) If you are bringing food or party goods, arrive whenever the hostess requests you be there.

(5) If you are giving a bridal or baby shower, please do not ask guests to write their own thank you note or address the envelope. The gift-giver took the time to shop, select, pay for and deliver the gift, and the recipient of the gift should show her appreciation by taking time to write a thank you note, address the envelope, stamp it, and put it in the mail.

Chapter Seven
Stop Smoking Now!
Above all else, guard your heart, for it is the wellspring of life.
Proverbs 4:23

Try to talk to others who have quit smoking successfully and find out what worked for them. Although TV advertisers want you to believe you cannot stop smoking "cold turkey" (just totally quit), that's how people used to do it before pills, patches, hypnosis, injections, etc. were available. Ask your friends for help, and ask God for help. Pray about it in earnest. Set a date, then do it.

Helpful hints to quit smoking:

• <u>**Change your habits**</u>. If you usually sit in a certain place and smoke while you are on the phone, sit somewhere else; keep a pencil and paper handy and draw/scribble while you talk. Stay away from people who smoke. If you smoke while driving, stop. Don't smoke in your house, and don't allow others to smoke inside. Brush your teeth often and enjoy the fresh taste in your mouth.

• <u>**Pacifiers**</u>. The urge for a cigarette only lasts about a minute. Be strong. Think about something else. Pretzels, carrot or celery sticks, gum, and mints will help. Buy Hershey's™ Kisses or other small candy to keep with you and in the freezer. *Small* is the key. Do not eat full sized candy bars as your reward. You will be unhappy with your weight gain and might start smoking again.

• <u>**Cut down**</u>. Reduce the daily number of cigarettes you smoke. If you smoke a pack, cut it to half. If you smoke a half, cut that in half. Make a serious effort to break the habit of picking up a cigarette without even thinking about it. The fewer cigarettes you smoke each day, the easier it is to quit.

• <u>**Try the *Tic Tac*™ Method**</u>. Every time you smoke, have one or two Tic Tacs afterward. Do this for about a week. Then, when you want a cigarette, have a Tic Tac instead. Your mind/body will think that you just finished a cigarette. By using this substitution, you will be able to cut back on your smoking and, hopefully, quit smoking.

- **Give yourself time**. Studies have shown it takes four weeks to break a bad habit or form a good one. Don't be too hard on yourself if you slide. Just keep trying. Set a "quit" date. You might need to do that more than once! Do not try to quit at a particularly stressful time, and never quit smoking and start a diet at the same time!

- **Afraid of gaining weight?** Start walking or begin an exercise program *before* you quit smoking. That has a dual benefit because when temptation arises, you can go for a walk or do some stretching exercises. Develop the habit of breathing deeply *without* the benefit of a cigarette!

- **Need more incentive?** Put a tissue over the filter end and inhale. The icky brown stain is the sticky tar that goes into your lungs with every puff.

- **Say positive things to yourself**. Look in the mirror and say, "I am not a smoker." "My mouth feels so fresh." "I can breathe deeply." Your mind will believe whatever you tell it.

- **Are you pregnant?** If you smoke while pregnant, your baby will be born addicted to nicotine and, once out of your body, the baby will go into withdrawal. All babies will cry to some extent, but a nicotine-addicted baby means LOTS of additional crying.

Once you quit, stay away from people who smoke and try this very effective exercise: when you want a cigarette, take a long, slow, deep breath. Smokers generally do not breathe deeply unless they are inhaling a cigarette. By taking deep breaths, your body is fooled into thinking you have smoked. This will help!

Also important – start a **Money I Saved By Not Smoking** jar. If you smoked a pack a day, then $4 (or more) goes into the jar each day. At the end of the month ($4 x 30 days), you will have saved $120. In three months, that's $360! One year equals $1,440! Not only that, but your lungs will immediately begin repairing themselves. Your skin will look better, and you will be a healthier person – with fewer wrinkles.

Use the money you saved by not smoking to reward yourself in some special way. Quitting smoking is a great achievement, and you should celebrate your success.

Chapter Eight
What's Your Attitude?
And we know that all things work together for good to those who
love God, those who are called according to His purpose.
Romans 8:28

Whether you are looking for job or personal advice, this chapter addresses both. Success in personal relationships is closely related to success in business.

As a stay-at-home mom for twenty-plus years, I have been there for my children, made money, and kept my sanity (for the most part). I have learned some tough lessons along the way, but the key was *learning*.

Choosing to be at home with the children instead of being a two-income family has not been an easy road financially. However, we felt the sacrifice was important for the growth of our children. Also, I have always managed to find some way to make money.

So, what can you do? How do you make money when jobs are scarce? How do you make money with a toddler at home? Find something you enjoy that other people need, and give some thought to the topics discussed in this chapter.

What is Your Attitude?

A friend of mine was talking about her brother who had recently passed away. "Oh, you would have loved him," she said. "He treated everyone so special. Regardless of who he was talking to, he made them feel like they were the most important person in the world." It was then I realized what was so special about her: she uses the same philosophy. I have watched her interact with people from all walks of life. Whether she is talking with a company president or a store clerk, she treats each person like they are a special gift. This woman is admired by all who know her.

Attitude can make or break you – in business as well as in personal relationships. If you tend to be a know-it-all who doesn't like to listen to others, it will be tough to be in business for yourself. A know-it-all attitude also alienates friends. Be aware of how you are perceived by others, and always listen more than you talk – especially if you always seem to be giving advice. If you think you might be talking too much, you are. Remember, nobody EVER learns anything while they are talking.

The Humble Spirit

Do you have a humble spirit? If you cannot listen to others without jumping in to give your (much better) story or opinion, the answer is no. If you always have something critical to say or sit in judgment of others, learn to keep your mouth shut. Train yourself to think positive thoughts – about everyone.

Are you a perfectionist and critical of others who don't share your beliefs? Don't confuse doing an excellent job with putting ridiculous demands on others and yourself. If people see you as a pushy know-it-all, chances are good that you will not have much success selling yourself.

Selling myself? Yes, along with selling a product, people will buy from you or hire you or spend time with you because they like *you* as well as your product or service.

Consider these points:
- *Kindness.* It doesn't cost anything extra to be nice.
- *Concern for others* (for their time as well as their feelings). When you approach others (whether a potential client, employer or friend), don't get lost in a long story and find them looking at their watch and making excuses to get away from you. If they decide you talk too much, you might not get a call back.
- *Have a pleasant disposition.* Don't always have a gripe to share. Nobody wants to hear it. We all have problems, but some folks seem to live from one catastrophe to the next. All they <u>ever</u> have are problems. If people seem to be avoiding you when you "need to talk," take a hint. No one likes to be captured by someone who talks on and on about themselves. Make your meeting a positive experience!
- *Smile.* Develop the ability (and peace within) to always have a pleasant, sincere smile on your face. Practicing in front of a mirror might be helpful.
- *Watch body language.* If someone's face turns "sour" after you have laughed, told a joke or said something that could be inappropriate, STOP TALKING and listen. Perhaps you can figure out what you did that was offensive. We are responsible for our behavior. Pay attention to signs from others and be open to change.
- *Straighten Up.* How's your posture? Do you slouch? Notice how successful people stand. They stand straight,

heads up, shoulders back. Think about politicians, heads of companies and people in positions of authority. Good posture immediately improves the way other people look at you and think about you.

Back up against a wall in your house. Make your shoulders, head, and heels touch the wall. Are you uncomfortable? Most people will find that position awkward. Do it several times a day and work on becoming more conscious of your posture. As your posture improves, you will notice that people look differently at you. Why? Because you look like you are somebody special!

Home Business – Put It On Paper

What do you want to do? Are you looking for a way to supplement your family income or are you thinking of starting a new business (possibly with a friend or your husband)? Make a list of things you enjoy and do well – or would enjoy learning. Having a job you truly enjoy makes every day a pleasure. Seeing your list on paper is different from just thinking about it. You should be very knowledgeable about the idea or product you want to market and, of course, you will continue to learn more.

Remember that many home businesses fail. Statistics show that about three fail to every four that start, so plan carefully. Success usually comes from recognizing a *need* and then filling it. Filling a need could mean a new concept, new product, or simply better customer service than the competition. Think about what you have to offer, available funds to start the business, your family, and your marketing strategy (advertising).

MORE THINGS TO CONSIDER
Family

If you want to start a new business, start by writing down your ideas. Be sure you consider how the business might affect your family. Will it make you inaccessible to your children? Will it take time away from your husband? Will you end up *needing* a wife instead of *being* one?

What about start-up expenses? Do you have money set aside? Are you planning to take money from the family funds? If so, this should be treated as a loan and repaid.

Dressing for Success

Regardless of the type work you do, you should be appropriately dressed. There is a big difference between *appropriate* and *expensive.* If you don't have "business" clothes, you can find great clothing at thrift stores or consignment shops – and possibly at your church if they have a clothes closet. Or place a wanted ad on www.freecycle.com. The type of business doesn't matter; people will give you more respect if you are nicely dressed. More than that, we tend to behave differently – more professionally – when we are dressed well.

What type of impression would your doctor make if he walked in wearing jeans and a t-shirt? What about your grocery store manager? Or the folks at your bank?

Wearing something nice makes you feel good about yourself. It helps you present yourself in a more positive way. Anyone can find a decent pair of pants or a skirt (knee length or longer) and a nice shirt or sweater (no sweatshirts, no t-shirts). Even a job that calls for jeans means clean, un-stained, newer-looking jeans.

If you're unsure, the rule for shirts is NO low cut (showing cleavage) or too short (belly-showing) shirts of any kind. Your shirt should have sleeves and a collar and should never be too tight – nor should skirts & dresses. Wear a slip with skirts and dresses (a half slip is fine). With a white shirt or blouse, wear a skin-toned bra (white bras under a white shirt scream, "Look, I'm wearing a bra!").

Hopefully, this is not an issue, but if you have chosen to have multiple ear piercings, other facial piercings, visible tattoos, unusual hair colors, etc. – your job options may be limited. Those things are considered odd and make others feel uncomfortable. In working with the public, you must fit in. Although there are exceptions, the basic rule for multiple piercings, visible tattoos, and other "new looks" is: *Successful people don't look like that.*

Spending Money Before You Make Money

Beware of the "I Need" money pit. If you are starting your business on a shoestring (practically no money), make it your goal to spend as little money as you can. Business cards are often a necessary expense; however, a new desk, new computer, all new office supplies, new phone – those are *wants*, not *needs*. A card table set up in the corner of your bedroom or kitchen might be the perfect home office for now. If you need a desk and filing cabinet, check the newspaper classifieds and the thrift stores. Make it a game. How little can you spend to get your business started? Place a WANTED ad for free items on craigslist.org or freecycle.com.

As your company begins to make money, you can look at improving your "office." Put a comfortable amount from each job into your business improvement fund. Don't forget to save money AND tithe.

If you have young children, you will need to make some provisions. There may be times when you can work around their naps, or your children might be good at amusing themselves for a while. But you cannot talk to clients while your child is demanding your attention. Whether it is a *Moms Morning Out* program, bartering childcare with a neighbor or paying for a few hours of childcare, you need to consider that expense and the planning it will involve.

One work-at-home mom had an embarrassing tale. The client was meeting her at home, where her two year old was playing quietly in another room. During their conversation, the male client was very distracted. When the mom finally turned around, she was horrified to see the contents of her lingerie drawer strewed about the room. It is fairly difficult to maintain an air of professionalism when you are competing with a two year old trying on bras.

When my daughter was in preschool, I worked from home. Mostly, I worked at night, but one day I simply *had* to get a job finished. After preschool, I sat her at a small table with markers and lots of paper. When I checked on her, she had colored her arm, finger tips to elbow, with permanent black marker. We quickly located suitable childcare, and my daughter enjoyed playing with other children when I needed time to myself.

A Word About SCAMS
Stuffing Envelopes and Assembling Crafts

DO NOT think for one moment that those "stuff envelopes for $$$'s" ads are legitimate. In the same category are the *assemble crafts, sewing, etc.* ads. These are SCAMS. While there are a few legitimate jobs in that line of work, they are hard to find. You generally won't find them in newspapers, in the back of magazines, or on the Internet. There are a *huge* number of scams running now, and more hit the papers and Internet every day.

Most of the Internet "opportunities" are scams. Do you really think a company is going to pay an unqualified person $1,000 a day to write ad copy for them? Of course not. If you *do* decide to check out Internet jobs, make a new email address – just in case you are bombarded with inappropriate ads, and <u>never</u> give out your real telephone number or any personal information unless you are dealing with a business you know is legitimate. (Use gmail.com, yahoo.com, aol.com, hotmail.com, etc. for free email addresses.)

If you are wondering about the validity of an opportunity, go to www.pueblo.gsa.gov and click on SCAMS/FRAUDS. You will be amazed at the list of fraudulent activities. Information on a variety of different subjects is also available on that website. Also, don't fall for "you have won the British lottery" or "help me move money out of the country." The first and most important rule is: *If it sounds too good to be true, it usually is.*

Second rule: Go with your "gut" feeling. First impressions are important. If something makes you suspicious or uncomfortable, <u>don't do it</u>. Don't doubt yourself.

Third rule: DO NOT pay anyone money. The idea is for you to MAKE money! When someone says, "Just send $10" (or any amount), a red flag should go up – don't do it. Exceptions are home party plans or MLM businesses (discussed in Chapter 9).

LEGALLY SPEAKING

I am not a lawyer, nor do I have certified legal training. For all legal questions, you should consult a lawyer, accountant or CPA as needed. That said, here is some basic advice:

Many of the suggested job ideas in Chapter 9 do not require a business license. You might need to get one but, especially in the beginning, you are trying to keep expenses low. If you need a business bank account, you may need a business license.

Have checks made out to your name and deposit them in your personal checking account, although a separate business account is helpful. You can operate out of a personal checking account and keep <u>good</u> records of all business deposits, receipts and expenses for tax purposes; however, it is helpful to have an accountant or CPA advise you as to exactly what can be deducted. For businesses that include cooking in your home, a business license might mean government inspections. Few folks could afford to install a commercial kitchen that meets OSHA regulations. Consult appropriate professionals for questions of this nature.

A word about prayer: pray that you will be led to do what God has planned for you. Pray the Prayer of Jabez, that God will enlarge your territory *(1 Chronicles 4:10)*. Ask others to pray for you, and pray for others.

Chapter Nine
Job Opportunities
*All hard work brings a profit, but mere talk leads
only to poverty. Proverbs 14:23*

*The ideas offered may not be successful in every area. Some might be better
suited to larger cities, others for small towns. Or perhaps the suggestions
might inspire you to come up with a great new idea. Read Chapter 8 for tips
on success. Advertising ideas are found on page 73.*

ABOUT BUSINESS CARDS
Business cards are generally a good investment for any type
of business. You will look more professional and people will be less
likely to lose your name and number. Choose a business name that
identifies what you do, or use your own name and identify your
business clearly on the card. *(See Naming Your Business, p.71.)*

If you are making business cards on your computer, look at
business card books at copy or printing shops to get ideas. Buy
business card paper at an office supply store or order from Paper
Direct (www.paperdirect.com).

ADDRESSING ENVELOPES
Many of us have seen this advertised. If you see an ad, you
can bet it's a scam (unless the ad is from your local card shop).
While there are real jobs addressing envelopes, they are rare. If you
want to pursue this possibility, you should contact stores involved in
any aspect of the wedding industry: shops that print invitations,
bridal shops, stores that rent tuxedos, florists, photographers, and
stationery stores like Hallmark.

Pricing: Ask at the stores to try to get an idea of what other
people charge. If no one else is offering that service, decide what
you can live with – maybe 10 to 15 cents per envelope. Or charge
more and offer an "Introductory Special" coupon (reduced prices).

If you have calligraphy skills, you can charge more. Also
charge more for full service (envelopes stuffed, stamped, sealed, and
mailed).

ARTS & CRAFTS CLASSES
If you are artsy and enjoy working with older children, you
might consider offering after school and/or home school classes.

Most children enjoy making crafts, and parents love their child to be safe and having fun in a positive, well-supervised environment.

A word about home schoolers: As the home school community grows, there is a greater need for extracurricular classes. Many moms are wizards when it comes to math and science but are lacking in the arts department. They are anxious to find *affordable* alternatives and might prefer their children be with other home schooled children. Although some home school families are comfortable financially, many are not. Families with three or more children would like ALL of the children to do special things – not just one. So keep your prices affordable!

One artist offered classes in her home for $10. The children brought their own art pad, pencils, erasers, and colored pencils. The teacher had no cash outlay and made anywhere from $100 to $150 for 1½ hours (with 10 – 15 children).

Children like to make crafts they are proud of, and parents get tired of ugly, useless crafts they can't easily throw away. Have the kids make something useful. Check the library for books that specialize in crafts for kids, and look on the Internet. Also, check www.michaels.com and www.joann.com.

Making and painting a birdhouse is always fun. If you can't use a saw, have someone cut the pieces for you. The children will nail them together, sand rough edges, and glue a perch in the pre-drilled hole you have made. Perhaps you can get creative with roofing materials. Have patterns, designs, or suggestions for painting the birdhouses. Finish with a clear, waterproof sealer.

Kits are available at craft stores or online, but look for someone to cut the wood for you to maximize your profits. A retired woodworker might welcome the chance to make a few dollars and offer good suggestions too! A local cabinet shop might be happy for you to haul away their wood scraps.

Investigate other easy-to-assemble craft projects. Pre-drill the holes and give the kids a screwdriver or hammer. Along with birdhouses and feeders, what about a simple garden bench? Or a small table with mosaic tile in the top? The children would have a grand time breaking tiles and using mortar to set the pieces!

Don't forget the ever popular paint your own T-shirt. Sponges pre-cut into shapes are great, and so are stencils. Put newspapers or a shirt-sized piece of cardboard inside the shirt so the paint won't go through. If you plan to re-use the cardboard for future classes, cover it with wax paper secured by masking tape.

Children have different levels of abilities. Some are very creative and need little assistance. Others might be overwhelmed by assembling something. They are generally willing to help each other, but plan other activities to keep the faster workers occupied.

Cooking classes for children are also popular. Of course, safety is a prime concern with cooking. You will need well-planned recipes so all the children are busy, and don't forget the plastic knives!

You might be able to advertise through your church. Look for other local online ways to get the word out. For home school groups, join several online loops for home schoolers. For the after school kids, advertise in neighborhood newsletters, church newsletters, or put flyers on mailboxes. Some schools might send flyers home with the kids. Think about offering a summer camp or holiday activity with seasonal crafts or special recipes – and perhaps a craft or cooking class for birthday parties.

BARTER / APPRENTICE

Money doesn't generally exchange hands with bartering, and the concept works quite well for some folks. For example, if you find another mom who needs childcare, you could swap out. Be careful to keep things even; no one wants to end up feeling used. Or perhaps that mom would like you to prepare dinner for her family in exchange for keeping your child.

Do you have a lot of pets and can't afford vet fees? Ask your vet if you could work it off. Cleaning kennel cages isn't fun but if it provides free pet care, you can handle a few hours! Or perhaps you could fill in as receptionist or file clerk.

Love to ride horses but can't afford to own one? Check with local stables and private owners about cleaning stalls or barn care in exchange for riding time or lessons. Be prepared for them to see you ride, and be *very* honest about your riding abilities. You don't want to get hurt.

Need free plants for your yard? Offer to help someone in their yard in exchange for plants. Ask a small nursery if they need some occasional help in exchange for plants or a good discount. When dealing with a business, make sure you get everything in writing so there is no misunderstanding later.

If you want to learn a new skill, take a job either as a volunteer (apprentice) or for less pay to learn the business. Examples: woodworker, caterer, mechanic, electrician, plumber, welder, etc.

BEFORE AND AFTER SCHOOL CARE

In many families, both parents work and younger children must get themselves to the bus on time. You could offer before school care – providing breakfast and making sure they get on the bus – and *after* school care where they will be safe, get a snack, have a place to do their homework, etc.

See DAYCARE for more information.

CHILDREN'S DANCE / CREATIVE MOVEMENT

When my second child was three years old, I began visiting local dance studios. My first child had taken ballet and tap at three years old; however, I was very disappointed at the recitals. The younger children did not have a grasp of the dance routine, and several stood on the stage sucking their thumbs. This wasn't just the three year olds; the four and five year olds were not much better. After seeing the same problem on videos from different studios, I decided I could do a better job.

I have no formal dance training. I took ballet and tap as a child and feel I have basic talent. Since I learn by watching, I borrowed beginning ballet videos from the library, and a friend made copies of her daughter's recital tapes because I wanted to see a variety of steps. Of great help in proceeding with this idea was that I truly believed this was what the Lord wanted me to do at that particular time.

From the time I first thought about it, it was a year before I felt ready to approach anyone to try to sell the idea. During that year, I made lists, wrote down ideas on how to teach as well as how the business part should work: how much to charge, days/hours, recital plans, etc. Finally, I was ready to talk to our church preschool director. She *loved* the idea. Without any dance credentials, I sold the idea and everything worked.

It also helped the preschool to have something else to offer to parents, giving the mothers another hour to themselves. *(This is a great example of identifying a need and filling it.)*

When you are working with children, you *must* keep things moving, and you *must* keep it interesting. You must have rules, and you must have fun. "My girls" were great. They listened, they learned, and they made me very, very proud. At our recitals, every single one of them danced! *For more information on how to start a dance program, see Appendix, page 174.*

COLLECTIONS

If you have ever been late paying a bill, you are familiar with collections! Unfortunately, there is a tremendous need for this type of service. It pays well and if your personality is right for the job, it might be perfect for you. There is also the option of working on your own, which would take a lot of persistence. You could set your own hours, but you might not see any money right away.

My friend was excellent at collections. Why? Because she had an understanding, helpful attitude with the clients. Her goal was to generate *some type* of payment. She made it personal, listening to the person's story of woe. Sometimes, she was able to negotiate a payoff by suggesting the client end this torment by coming up with half of the money, maybe less. It depended on what the collections agency would accept.

If you choose this line of work, know up front that you will not be a popular person. People with Caller I.D. may not answer their telephones. Some of us take rejection very personally while it just doesn't bother others as much. Know yourself before taking this type of job. If you don't enjoy what you do, it isn't worth the money. If you are interested in this line of work, there are helpful sites online that give information, but *do not pay* for courses. It would be best to work for a collections agency so you could learn about the details of the job before starting your own business. Also, you would have experience to offer as you sell yourself to other companies who need to collect bad debts.

COMPUTERS
Teaching Classes

Computer classes are springing up everywhere, and each class needs a teacher. It is a perpetual job market: preschools that teach simple games to children, individuals willing to pay for one-on-one instruction, evening classes/community schools, classes that teach folks how to build and/or repair their own computer, computer companies that install new systems and need instructors to teach their employees, and don't forget our seniors!

More and more senior citizens are interested in learning to use the computer so they can email friends and family. Many churches and Senior Centers offer computer classes for seniors.

Prepare a letter and/or resume introducing yourself and visit these places in person. You can also place a free ad under "Services" on www.craigslist.org for this and most of the other jobs listed.

Finding Computer Work

To find part-time computer work, make a flyer or write an introduction letter and visit offices to advertise for temporary work. If you have little experience, you will be learning "on the job." Salary depends on your level of experience, but starting pay for no experience is usually minimal. **Take free computer classes online at www.gcflearnfree.org.**

COOKING

Can you make wonderful cakes? The grocery stores do a good job, but there is nothing like a freshly baked, homemade cake. You could make cakes and pies (and perhaps other yummy desserts) and deliver them – something retail stores cannot offer – and busy folks appreciate things that save them time. Consider making special desserts for diabetics and people with wheat/gluten allergies!

Make flyers and distribute in neighborhoods. If a sub-division has a newsletter, advertise in it. If you specialize in decorated cakes, make some good pictures and put them in a small photo album to show to prospective clients.

What about biscuits? There may be local businesses or convenience stores that would *love* to serve real homemade biscuits. Make a batch of biscuits, figure out the best way to keep them warm, and visit potential clients with your hot, homemade samples – don't forget the butter, jellies, napkins, and plastic knives! Give out business cards or flyers with your name, phone number, and the items you cook.

Small event catering is another needed service. Church or sports dinners, office luncheons or meetings, and neighborhood events could be clients. Plan and price carefully. Catering is hard work, and you want to make sure to make a profit.

Cooking can be done in your *very* clean kitchen; however, OSHA frowns on people preparing food in their homes. If you cook for others, be cautious. Don't let the newspaper do an article on you!

CRAFTS

There are different categories of crafts. There are home-made crafts that *really* look homemade. In fact, they look so home-made they should never be given as gifts. You may offer them to others, or you may try to sell them, but DO NOT give them as gifts. It is most awkward to receive an unwelcome gift that you feel obligated to display. Check out www.michaels.com for craft ideas.

Selling Your Crafts

- Pick one basic area where you are the most talented and devote your energy to making that line the very best. If you spread out into too many areas, you might become frustrated and not end up finishing anything. Visit craft shops, flea markets, county fairs, etc. and see what appears to be selling best in your area. Talk to the crafters and see what tips you can pick up.

- Local merchants might be willing to display some of your items. Make sure you are clear on the terms: the store might buy your things outright or have a 50/50 split (or better). Perhaps the store is owned by a friend who will give you all the profit. Don't forget about eBay and craigslist.org.

- Check the Internet and craft magazines for ideas, and watch for opportunities. Quality Christian crafts have a market. Churches and schools have craft shows or fall festivals where you can rent a booth to display your goods.

Christmas Craft

Most folks love the smell of evergreens during Christmas. A wonderful way to decorate your home is to visit Christmas tree lots and ask for free tree trimmings. Smaller lots might use the trimmings to make wreathes or garland while larger stores (like Home Depot & Lowe's) will trash their trimmings. Each year, they are happy for folks to haul off free branches. You will need containers (buy at yard sales or dollar stores), oasis foam (holds water), <u>waterproof</u> florist tape (buy at craft store, florist or online), and candles to make your own arrangements. They are great for teacher and neighbor gifts, or you could sell them.

To make these arrangements, you need a sturdy plastic or glass container (1-2 inches deep by 4-6 inches across) to hold the foam. Cut a piece of foam to fit the container; you should be able to cut three equal-sized pieces from a block. The foam should be at least one inch taller than the bowl. Soak foam in water before putting it into the bowl. Hold foam in place with two strips of waterproof tape. Run tape from one side of the container to the other to hold the foam in place. Tape strips should be long enough to overlap the container by at least one inch on both sides. *(See example)*

In the center, place a taper (tall, thin) candle or use other decoration (like a nutcracker or child-safe ornament) if you don't want candles. During the holidays, you can find tapers on sale.

For a medium-sized arrangement, cut your bottom branches about ten inches long. Insert branches about an inch into the sides and ends of the foam to form the base of your arrangement. Angle the bottom branches down to cover your container. As you work your way up to the candle, use shorter branches, maybe only a few inches long when you are filling in the area right around the candle. Make sure you hide all of the foam. Finish your arrangement with colorful "picks" from the craft store, ting-ting, or whatever appeals to you.

Fresh flowers add a special touch. Use Baby's Breath, mini-carnations, or mums. Roses are beautiful, but they won't last as long as the other flowers. Berries are pretty (holly, nandina or other), and you can also add different greeneries. For balance, use three of each flower you choose (like three red carnations and three white ones) – or use three decorative picks if you are not using flowers. Using decorative picks and Baby's Breath is a very nice combination.

Use an oblong container and a full brick of oasis to make a larger arrangement with three tapers. Visit craft stores and florist shops and look at pre-made arrangements for more ideas!

DAYCARE BUSINESS

This will allow you to be at home and available (somewhat) to your own children. Check to see what other daycares are charging. Get a book from the library or talk to people who have done this. You will need strict rules, nap-time places for each child, and planned meals and snacks. Decide how early you will accept children and how late they will stay. You will need information sheets on each child, including detailed medical info.

New germs will be coming into your home. Especially if your child has not been in a preschool environment, you and your child may get sick from exposure to the new germs. You might need booster shots; ask your doctor. Clean toys and blankets daily. Teach the children to wash their hands often, to use tissues, and to always cover their mouths when they sneeze (then wash the germs off their hands). Keep a well-stocked first aid kit.

How will your children accept strangers in their house? Playing with their toys? Buy "new" (used/garage sale) toys that are kept separate from your child's toys and sanitize them. You may need to keep all bedrooms off limits to visitors.

Find a helper who would come in each day or maybe only on days when you need more help. Remember, you will have occasional doctor and dentist visits for your own children, as well as other errands that must be done during "work" hours.

Another option would be to provide *only* before and after school care. The children might arrive as early as 6am. You would provide breakfast. They would return (by bus) after school. You would provide a snack, perhaps a second snack or dinner if the parents don't pick them up before 6pm.

Do lots of research and write everything down. Parents will need to sign some sort of agreement; that seems to make people more responsible. Prepare a form to get their address and ALL telephone numbers and health insurance information. Talk with your homeowner's insurance company to see if there are any stipulations or additional fees for running this type of business from your home. If someone is injured on your property, you must be protected.

eBAY SELLING

It's a giant marketplace. Library books have helpful hints. If you are computer savvy, go to www.ebay.com and easy-to-follow instructions will get you started. You need a decent digital camera and the ability to upload pictures. Each listing costs money (relative to the price of your item), whether you sell your item or not. It is a bit of a gamble but can pay off with persistence. See what is selling. On left side of eBay screen, click on *Completed Listings;* also check into buying *Lots*, which you would separate and sell individually. Volume is the key to success. Keep it honest. eBay takes a serious interest in ethical practices and will pursue offenders.

eBay can be a gamble. We sold a four-station gym and were willing to take a loss, just to get it out of our house. We put it up for auction (local pick-up only) with a low starting price. One person bid and bought the $400 gym for $10. We felt bad until we learned he was a small town preacher who felt he had received a miracle. He even felt guilty about his good fortune.

Whether you are buying or selling, the excitement of an auction ending is great fun – especially if you are winning! eBay is a great place to sell many items (but not all), and timing matters.

HANDYGALS

At some point, almost everyone needs a handyman. But there aren't enough to go around! They are either too busy, too expensive, or they don't want to do small jobs. Travel time for a small (low paying) job means they could spend the same amount of time traveling to a big job and make $800+ compared to the $300 you are going to make. Depending on how much money you need, you could work one day a week while the children are in school.

Some of us are not gifted with hammers nor with anything electrical, so we should not pursue this type of work. However, there are a lot of women who are very talented in this area. Some jobs might be limited because of the physical strength required, but there are *many* smaller jobs that women could do as a *Handygal.*

One lady desperately needed someone willing to do small jobs. The screens on her porch were flapping; her wallpaper needed to be replaced, and she needed other routine maintenance. Unfortunately, she had to depend on friends to help here and there, because the jobs were not big enough to attract a handyman.

Women and elderly folks might be more comfortable having a woman in their home to do repairs. There are many elderly people who need light fixtures and ceiling fans installed or replaced, minor wood and sheetrock repairs, doorbells fixed, a "peep hole" installed – the list goes on and on. Changing out a chandelier seems like a big deal, but have you ever seen that done? It takes no time at all – but you have to know what you're doing and know how to work with electricity.

Another big market is people who have the money but not the time (nor desire) to do the work. There are homeowners wanting to get houses ready for sale and people who have rental properties. This is a *huge* market. Once your name gets out, you might have more work than you ever wanted! People are always asking others if they know anyone who does small jobs. Referrals are the best advertising.

If you think you have basic skills in this area but are not quite sure of yourself, find a handyman who is willing to answer your questions and help sharpen your skills. Make sure he knows how to do small electrical work. Perhaps he will let you ride with him on a few calls. Learn to do doorbell work, indoor and outdoor fixtures, etc. Since you will be advertising for small jobs that he doesn't want to bother with, you won't be competition. He might even send you business!

Get business cards. The cards should say exactly what you do, like "Small Jobs by Suzie." Then, in smaller print, list some of the things you do: screens repaired, ceiling fans installed, light fixtures and faucets replaced, doorbell repair, sheetrock repair, etc.

One other note: be safety conscious. If you are working for a single woman or an elderly couple, that is probably a pretty safe situation. If you are working alone, be cautious. Keep doors locked and, basically, if someone makes you uncomfortable, don't brush it off as being silly. Listen to your "gut" feeling. Be careful – and don't take any chances. Keep a cell phone with you.

HOME PARTY/HOME BUSINESS

There are a number of companies who recruit folks to sell by "party plans." The hostess invites her friends and provides refreshments. You show your product line and collect the orders. Sound simple? It really is. It is a great money-making idea for some folks. Examples of party plan companies would be Tupperware, Pampered Chef, Home Interiors, etc.

Although I have sold for several different "party plan" companies, selling does not seem to be my calling. I just couldn't seem to make it. But everyone is good at something; it might be perfect for you. There will be a start-up fee of $30-100+ for most companies. This gives you enough products to start selling. It is also important to have a good director to encourage you.

For true success in the home party business, it helps to know A LOT of people: relatives, friends, PTA, church, Sunday School class, etc. Your friends/family can help you get started.

With MLM (multi-level marketing) companies, you must recruit others to sell "under" you. This gives you a commission from their sales. You can approach friends, but do not get angry if they don't share your enthusiasm. It is better to recruit strangers and preserve your friendships! MLMs usually require a minimum monthly purchase of $50 or more. From personal experience, most MLMs seem to make money off of the representatives and, regardless of the sales pitch, few reps actually make a decent profit unless, perhaps, they make selling an active full time job.

Through the Internet, more home-based business opportunities are available. Although some are legitimate, you will find people who would take your last dollar and feel no remorse. Check out the company as much as possible before you commit. *Don't commit if you can't afford to lose the money.*

HOUSE CLEANING & MORE

Everyone knows about cleaning houses, but what about cleaning offices? Or construction clean-up (new subdivision houses). You must visit the offices or construction sites to ask about availability and pay. When you accept a job, be sure you are clear on all details; write it down and have them sign it. Word of mouth is the least expensive way to advertise, and it is the best way to ensure your safety.

Housecleaning is one of the easiest ways to supplement your income. Call around to see what others are making and how much work they actually do. Hand out business cards to everyone.

MOM'S TAXI

This is a shuttle service for children – such a great example of identifying a need, and then filling it. Some working parents can't take their children to music or dance lessons, sports practice, etc. but would love for their child to participate. What if you could take these children to and from their lessons/activities each week?

What to charge? Consider gasoline costs and extra insurance. You might need a chauffeur's license. Investigate fully before you start your business. If you charge too much, you won't have any business. Hopefully, you will have several children to drop off and pick up, so you will end up making decent money for your time. Remember, you will only be working from whatever time the schools release to maybe eight o'clock. Summertime and other school breaks should present additional opportunities.

To advertise, try leaving flyers or business cards at doctor and dentist offices. Ask at school offices, you might be able to send a flyer home with the children. Perhaps the library or grocery store has a bulletin board where you could put a flyer. Better still, have a magnetic sign made for the back of your vehicle (and/or one for each side, if you can afford it). Don't make it too "busy" – a descriptive name and large, easy-to-read telephone number is all you need. Keep business cards or flyers in your vehicle so you can quickly give information to anyone who is interested.

OFFICE HELP

There are small companies that need part-time help. Some might need a person one or two days a week; others might want to call only when they have a specific need. "Small company" usually means independently-owned businesses. Florists are extra busy during prom season and major holidays. Accounting firms need extra help from January through April 15. Other companies might be busy with end of the month reports. Once you work successfully for one local company, you then have a reference to give to the next one.

IMPORTANT: Before you make this choice, know your strengths. Do you have good grammar skills and a pleasant telephone voice? Are you good at alphabetizing (for filing)? Do you know your way around basic office procedures/machines? Do not say you can do something that you really cannot do. It will make things awkward because they will have to fire you.

Do you need to work certain hours or are you flexible? Can they call you *only* when they need extra help, or do you need to know you will be paid each week for a certain number of hours? Maybe they only need help when an employee is out sick, has a sick child, or is on vacation. Figure out what you need/want, and then make your pitch to prospective employers.

Prepare a short, introductory letter. *(See sample on page 177.)* Make sure you have someone read the letter *before* you make copies – or read it out loud to catch errors. Use good grammar and be sure everything is spelled correctly. Sign each letter (do not photocopy your signature); put each one in a business-sized envelope (called a #10), and go to office parks or businesses near your home. Go door to door and tell them you are looking for part-time work. If they don't have a need at that time, ask if you can leave your letter. Ignore "No Soliciting" signs. You have no idea how many off-the-street vendors try to sell things in offices. You are offering a <u>service</u>. If someone is mean, you don't want to work there anyway.

PAINTING

People are always looking for good interior house painters. This could be a great job for a two-woman (or husband/wife) team.

Specialty painting, those who do faux finishing and mural painting, is another great option. Themes painted on the walls of children's rooms are always popular for younger children. Even if you aren't the best artist, a picture placed on an overhead projector lets anyone draw an object to the desired size. You must be a creative painter to make this work! You could begin by decorating and painting wall themes on some rooms in your house or in your finished garage or basement. Make pictures of your finished work so you will have samples to show prospective clients.

PET SITTING

Especially if you live in an area of subdivisions, this can be a most lucrative endeavor. Try to find out what other pet sitters in your area are charging. An Internet search might be helpful, and check with local veterinarians and kennels to see what they charge for boarding. Keep your rates competitive.

Many pet owners would rather leave their pets at home instead of in cages at the vet's office. For home care, a fair rate might be $15 per trip to let out and feed 1-2 dogs. Depending on the prices in your area, additional animals could raise the rate a few dollars. The homeowner might want you to bring in the mail and newspapers. Don't charge extra for that!

Another need is by single folks who work long hours and would like their dog to get out during the day.

If your business really starts growing, find a responsible person to help you. If you have ten separate clients to feed and let out over a four day weekend (let's say all dogs), that's $120 per job. So, $30 (2 trips per day @ $15 each) x 4 days x ten jobs = $1,200. If all of your customers are located within your subdivision, it is manageable. But if you're working a larger area, and perhaps want to be home to enjoy Christmas morning, find an assistant who would like to make some extra money.

Make sure you keep a good calendar. Forgetting a client could be disastrous – for your business and for the homeowner's carpet! Advertise by putting flyers on mailboxes and community bulletin boards. Some subdivisions have newsletters – a great place to advertise. Tell your friends, and hand out business cards. You might need to check into becoming "bonded" – to protect yourself while inside the homes of others. Do your research online: google *dog sitters* and include the name of your town or county.

PHOTOGRAPHY

If you make great pictures, you could make money. This job was moderately successful for me. Until I can afford a high-end digital, I am using a Nikon N-80 SLR because I think it offers good creativity. Much of this section will be about SLRs; however, there are many photo tips that will be helpful to digital users.

For SLR practice film, check online. Expiration dates don't matter if film has been refrigerated. Buy 100 or 200 ASA for cleaner enlargements. Never buy higher than 400 ASA if the grain is going to matter.

To develop your portfolio, find a "model" (kids & teenagers love to have their pictures made) to accompany you to a local park or other places of interest. Make pictures in different types of light. Try putting your subject in front of a window (stained glass is nice) and don't use a flash. Or pose them at sunrise or twilight on a hill with only the sun rising or setting behind them. Silhouettes can be fabulous. Outside, have your model lean on a fence rail, against a tree, building, barn, large rock, etc. Experiment with different poses, with flash and without, and see what works best. To solicit wedding photography work, your portfolio will need wedding photos.

For SLRs, have your pictures developed at a place that will accept rejects. When you have your pictures developed, study them to see what you did wrong and give back the ones you don't want. If you don't want ANY of the photos or the negatives, you can usually turn in the entire package and pay nothing at all. Ask the store about their policy – don't just assume it will work that way. Particularly if the store knows you will be bringing your business there, they should be more willing to work with you.

Since this is an area where I have a fair amount of experience, I will share the things I've learned. This is a lengthy section, so please refer to the *Appendix* (pages 178-182) for details. Even if you don't decide to take up photography as a job, you might find good tips to improve your personal photography.

REAL ESTATE FLYERS
For many years, I made money creating real estate flyers. Mostly, it was resale homes. Sometimes my client would want a new subdivision flyer with five or six small pictures of the different models of homes available. And there was the occasional open house or agent luncheon flyer.

Then, technology improved and just about everybody had a computer and a program that would create flyers. I didn't think their programs did as good a job as I did and I knew I was more meticulous in my spelling, grammar, and general detail – but it didn't matter; I still lost the business.

However – if this is something you might like to pursue, something that might work in your area, take these steps:
  (1) Find samples of other real estate flyers. Many times, agents have a flyer info box outside the home.
  (2) Prepare some "dummy" flyers to show different borders, fonts, and layouts. Use fake names and numbers.

(3) *Prepare an order form, run off copies, and take them to the real estate offices. My form had designated places for all info about the house on the front side and copies of reduced dummy flyers on the back.*

Make enough copies to put a form in each agent's mailbox. Call the office to ask how many agents work there. You would never know it, because many work from home, but there might be more than eighty agent mailboxes in an office (in larger suburban areas).

What to charge? You need to check the going rate in your area. Keep your prices competitive. Offer an "Introductory Coupon" or "This price good through ____" (pick a date). Ask the office manager if that office prepares flyers "in house" (in the office) or if the agents use outside sources. Also ask the manager how much they pay if flyers are out-sourced. It is best to ask in person.

RUNNING ERRANDS/COURIER/PERSONAL ASSISTANT

This idea would seem best for more heavily populated areas because more women will be working, and women could be your primary customers. Fewer people are doing this, so it will be harder to determine rates. Based on what you think people in your area would pay, charge $15 or $20 an hour (or a per trip fee), plus mileage if considerable travel is involved. The idea is to build up your business to where you are shopping or traveling for several clients in that same hour. So instead of making $15 an hour, you're actually making much more! *I saw an ad for this recently; she charged $45 for 2 hours and $100 for eight hours.*

There is potential in this idea, but it will also require some thought as far as whether to deal only in cash or if you pay with your personal check and then collect a check from them. Be careful; you don't want to collect a bad check. You might want to deal entirely in cash if you have any questions about your client. Use good judgment and don't go on blind faith.

At Christmas, working moms might welcome the opportunity to have gifts bought and safely tucked away at home rather than fighting evening and weekend crowds. Business people might be interested in someone who would shop for (and possibly wrap, mail, or deliver) gifts for their business associates.

Advertise through churches, craigslist.org, subdivision newsletters, and by handing out flyers to offices. A magnetic sign for your car (Personal Shopper or Personal Assistant) could be effective. Have a business card ready to hand out to everybody you meet.

SEASONAL DECORATING / PARTY PLANNER

As the name implies, this job is not a steady moneymaker. You might need lots of contacts/friends to make this work – but how much fun! In a nice neighborhood ($300,000's), a lady paid $300 to someone who came and used the homeowner's decorations to "dress the house" for Christmas. That price also included taking the decorations down and repacking them after the holidays.

Party Planning is taking the idea one step further. Developing a menu and purchasing food, decorations, and party supplies would fill a great need for professional women and working moms.

This could include decorating/planning theme parties, birthday parties (children and adult), Halloween parties, Halloween yard decor, etc. Some folks are not creative or just don't have enough time. They would be happy to pay someone to decorate and/or plan their party. And they will be happy to refer you to their friends.

How to charge? If you are interested in this type of work, you might have friends and contacts who could advise you. Regarding the decorating job mentioned above, this was for a nice, not overly large home. The price probably included décor and arrangements for the living room, dining room, family room, kitchen, powder room, etc. For larger houses, maybe $500,000 and up, your price might be $500 - $600. If decorated Christmas trees are wanted throughout the house (I knew of a home that had ten), make sure you figure in the time to decorate and repack everything.

Figure in your "creative" time (planning/ideas), shopping time, and the time you will spend physically decorating for the party – including locating appropriate serving dishes (purchased or belonging to the client). Make it worth your time but also a good price for the client. Business cards are a necessity. Word of mouth referrals are invaluable.

SEWING

Do you enjoy sewing? Are you good at it? If you are a bit rusty, take a refresher course through a fabric store or a community program. Sewing seems to be headed toward extinction. People will throw away clothing because they can't repair a hem or split seam. Some can't sew on a button.

You could advertise simple mending (hand and machine) and probably do quite well. This would include hemming pants, skirts and jacket sleeves, sewing split seams, and general mending. If you can replace a zipper, that's even better!

Alterations require more skill, but there is always a great need for those services. Or how about low- or no-sew drapes and designer pillows? For pricing, think about the time involved or use the *cost of materials x 3* rule. If you do not know someone who does this and could share information, call places that advertise alterations and ask what they charge for different services. Another untapped niche is making costumes – for kids and adults.

Make flyers and distribute on mailboxes, community bulletin boards, <u>craigslist.org</u>, churches, and place ads in subdivision newsletters. It would also be good to have business cards to give to everyone you meet.

TEACHING – no degree necessary

Do you enjoy teaching or showing others how to do things? Would you like to teach but don't have a degree? Or maybe you have a degree but don't want a full time job? Here's a way to fulfill that teaching urge and make money too!

In some areas, there are "community school" programs. These classes are held at night in local high schools. If your area doesn't have anything like that, you might be able to work out something with a local church, library, or other community building.

Think of things you do well enough to teach. It could be one night, two nights, or a six week (one night a week) course. The key is the number of people who sign up. The school (or church) may charge a fee. But if you have a one night course for $15 per person and 10 people sign up, you have made $150 (less the building rental/administrative fee) for two to three hours of work. *Get info on the administrative fee up front. In my community school, the school gets half of the registration fee.*

If there isn't anything you do well enough to teach, but you think you would really enjoy teaching, find a course you enjoy and learn something well enough to teach it! Don't sell yourself short. Somehow, I thought that if *I* knew how to do it, everyone else knew how to do it, too. That isn't true, friends. Get out there and share your knowledge with others!

If you are unsure about being in front of a group, practice in front of a mirror or practice on a friend, your husband, or your children. If you are nervous, perhaps "team teaching" would be a good way to start, or have a friend or your older child there for moral support. Find what works for you!

Check out the ideas on the following page:

Teaching Ideas
knitting, crocheting, quilting
basic sewing
upholstery basics
organizing your household
dancing or a particular type of dance – jazz, tap, ballet, ballroom,
          creative movement, line dancing, etc.
exercise – for the physically fit, for seniors, pregnant moms, etc.
Tai Chi, Karate, Yoga
tennis – separate classes for adults and children
babysitting for 11 years old and up (teach first aid, basic cooking,
          games, how to straighten the house a bit, etc.)
cake decorating
canning classes (using a pressure cooker, prep work, etc.)
catering – getting started, tricks of the trade
cooking classes for kids
cooking classes for adults
drawing, painting, and/or craft classes for kids
photography
digital photography
computer – beginner through advanced courses
painting – watercolor, acrylic, or oil
calligraphy
drawing
wallpapering, painting, faux finishing & stenciling
scrapbooking
how to sell on eBay
floral arranging
making gift baskets
CPR
setting up and maintaining an aquarium
creating and maintaining a backyard pond
basic landscaping, plant selection
dog obedience training
guitar lessons
foreign languages
sign language
automobile maintenance
basic woodshop skills (if school does not have a woodshop, you
          could demonstrate using different types of nails, screws,
          saws, drills, a miter box, etc. – or build a fancy birdhouse!)

Children's Classes

Although many of the above-mentioned classes could also be offered to children, other ideas are age-appropriate art classes, "home alone" classes, and "manners" – a children's tea party where they would learn about setting a table and appropriate behavior at a dinner party, greeting adults, etc. Remember, when teaching children, you *must* make it fun as well as a learning experience. If the children have fun, they will tell their friends!

TELECOMMUTING (work from home)

Go to http://workathomemoms.about.com. Scroll down the page; under "Browse," click on **Work-at-Home Jobs.** There is good info on the site and jobs listed. Read carefully before you click on any of the advertising. *This website has already changed during the editing of this book, so the information might be different than listed.*

WORK AT SCHOOL

Private and public schools need substitute teachers; many schools only require a high school diploma. Driving a bus works well for some moms (and dads); some school districts offer bus drivers a good salary plus full benefits. Working as a lunch lady offers fewer hours but may provide full benefits. Once you get in the system, you have the option of switching to a different job. This is great for many moms with school-aged children because they are working the same hours and days their children are away from home.

WRITING

Your library should have the **Writers Market Guide**, which lists many sources and ideas. Along with publishing books and magazine articles, there are listings for greeting card companies, writing contests, and more. If you are good with cartoon-type drawings and have a great sense of humor, there is a good market for humorous greeting cards. Card companies are always looking for new ideas. You might want to join a writing group. Always be cautious about opportunities advertised on the Internet.

OTHER THINGS TO CONSIDER
Naming Your Business

The name you choose will reflect your self-confidence and your business attitude. It is best to choose a name that identifies what you do and that sounds professional.

Be careful. If you are going with a "cutesy" name or some type of play on words, get the opinion of others (professional people) before you proceed. I recently saw "PMS" in BIG letters on the back of a truck. In smaller letters, it spelled out "Pool Maintenance Service. To me, that was offensive. If I had a pool, I absolutely would not use a company that felt the need to poke fun at something personal. If I find it offensive, others probably do too. When choosing a name, do it with care. Don't alienate potential customers by choosing a questionable name.

Customer Service

Word of mouth advertising is best. That means happy customers have told their friends. You are getting free advertising WITH a reference.

Remember, attitude is everything. Years ago, there was a saying: *The Customer is Always Right*. You don't see that attitude as much today. But YOU are a small business, one that cares about the customer, cares about doing a good job, cares about good referrals, and who truly is interested in having a happy customer – because that is how you are going to make money and grow your business.

There is no greater feeling than doing a good job and seeing the happy look on your customer's face. Many times, it is the look of surprise – because you did what you said you were going to do, with the quality you promised, and you did it when you said you were going to do it. Sometimes, the customer is totally shocked. Sadly, many of us are used to people who will take our money and have no regard for what they are giving us.

Remember: *you cannot please everybody all of the time.* There will be times when you have done your job perfectly, but the client is just in a bad mood. Some people simply cannot be pleased, and others will pick your work apart as a game to see how much you will cut your price. If a client seems overly picky at the first meeting or phone call, you might want to politely refuse the job. It won't get any easier. You don't need the stress – or the aggravation – of dealing with people who are going to give you a hard time and want something for nothing.

Never be rude. Don't get trapped in someone else's hateful attitude. And do not talk down to others – *ever*. Particularly if you really want to make it in a service-related industry, a good attitude is just as important as skill!

Advertising Your Services – On Paper & More

Flyers are generally a good advertising tool. Use white or yellow paper with black ink. Print from your computer or check prices at a copy shop. It might be cheaper to go to a copy shop than to run your printer cartridge dry. Read it out loud and try to get someone else to read it before you print it. Glaring mistakes can appear AFTER you spend the money to have it printed, even when you proofread it five times! Make sure you *also* read headlines. Use large print and make it interesting – but professional. Do not make it too "busy"; white space on the page is preferable to too much print or too many graphics (pictures).

Business cards are usually a good idea. Give one to everybody you meet! *See page 52 for more information.*

Some businesses benefit from a magnetic sign on the car door. The sign should say your business name and telephone number large enough for people to read at a distance, and it could have a small graphic. With a magnetic sign, you are advertising your services every time you drive your car. Check into possible tax deductions for using your personal vehicle as an advertising source, and keep plenty of business cards and/or flyers handy.

Other advertising options might be your church bulletin board, church classifieds paper, distributing flyers to adult Sunday School classes, Moms Morning Out groups, pre-school parents, subdivision newsletters, bulletin boards in the community, etc. Most of the jobs mentioned in this chapter could be advertised free on craigslist.org. When using craigslist, use a different email address from your main one, don't list a telephone number in your ad, and be cautious of any strange wording in the responses. Generally, sincere people will provide a telephone number. **WEBSITES**: create a great website on godaddy.com for around $10 a month. The site is very user-friendly, and their technical support staff is American!

Constructive Criticism – A Valuable Tool

When you are getting started in a new field, it is helpful to find someone who is knowledgeable and can offer constructive criticism. Remember there is a big difference between constructive criticism and someone who is critical. Critical people can destroy your confidence – and your dreams.

Be patient. Be prepared for the time it takes to develop your ideas and gain experience. Surround yourself with positive people. Give yourself time to learn, and don't be afraid to live your dream!

Chapter Ten
Get Ready to Cook
This is what the Lord Almighty says: "Give careful thought to your ways." Haggai 1:5

Meals and Manners

Meal time is a special time in my family. We eat together almost every night and have a big dinner after church almost every Sunday. Especially on Sunday, everyone is expected to know how to act at the table. Sometimes we eat in the dining room with a formal table setting where we use the good china, crystal glasses, cloth tablecloth and cloth napkins.

Children should know what it means when two forks are placed to the left of the plate. It's embarrassing to go to a nice restaurant where they (loudly) exclaim, "Hey, somebody left two forks here!" A simple table setting and a more formal setting appear below. The "formal" setting does not include all the pieces, just the ones most frequently used.

Simple Setting   *Modified Formal Setting*

The simple setting is self-explanatory. If you use napkin rings, place the napkin to the left of the fork or in the center of the plate. Or use a nicely folded napkin (cloth or paper) under the fork. The folded edge of the paper or cloth napkin should be next to the plate. Cloth napkins add elegance to the table. Plates and flatware are placed one inch from the edge of the table. Flatware refers to eating utensils (knife, fork, etc.).

For the modified formal setting, items such as the fish fork, fish knife, and the red and white wine glasses have been omitted. If you need to set *that* formal of a table, I am certain you have an etiquette book!

Formal Setting: From the left, you have a salad fork, dinner fork, charger plate (or dinner plate), dinner knife, and teaspoon. If you are serving soup, your soup spoon will be between the knife and teaspoon. Your dessert spoon and/or fork will be at the top of the plate. A bread and butter plate (or salad plate if you are not serving in "courses") is placed at the upper left.

A charger plate is an oversized plate that basically holds the dinner plate. If you were to serve in courses, the soup bowl would be brought to the table first and placed on the charger. Then the soup bowl would be removed, and the salad plate would be placed on the charger, and so on. According to one expert, the charger "holds the place" and "keeps the table from looking bare."

Basic Table Manners

- Put your napkin in your lap. If you get up, leave it in your chair. When the meal is over, leave it on the table.
- Don't eat until everyone is seated and served.
- If you must blow your nose or cough a lot, leave the table.
- Do not clink flatware on glass plates.
- Chew with your mouth closed; don't talk when there is food in your mouth, and don't slurp soup or drinks.
- When you drink, take sips – no "chugging."
- Push your chair in when you leave the table.

Meat & Potatoes Meals

For years, friends have loved our meals – not because the food is fancy but because it is simple. The recipes are based on the traditional "meat & potatoes" idea and are home-cooked rather than coming from a box.

As a reader of all types of self-help books and articles, I was always drawn to flashy headlines and suggested lists. "Just do this and your problems will be over" never seemed to work for me. There were lots of wonderful recipes my children wouldn't eat and helpful hints like "Plan your menu weeks in advance" – good advice but not if you eat according to what is on sale that week.

By centering menus around a certain number of items, it saves money and time. You have probably seen *plan your wardrobe* articles where you buy clothing in three or four coordinating colors.

From that, you have a seemingly endless number of mix and match outfits. Along the same line, if you stock a supply of "staple" items, you can make a number of different dishes from what is in the pantry. These ingredients are not exotic foods, just the meat and potato/rice/pasta dishes that most of us love. That keeps expenses down, helps frayed nerves, and you don't have to come up with imaginative meals unless you're just feeling creative!

Although most of us are trying to be more health conscious these days, there are times when you might need to be more concerned with saving money – or possibly just finding something your children will eat. These recipes may not be the healthiest meals ever, but they are NOT filled with fat, chemicals or preservatives and are healthier than most processed foods.

Processed foods are frozen dinners, "cheese foods," "dinner in a box," etc. Look at the list of ingredients. If it lists things you cannot pronounce, do you really want to eat them? For example, it just doesn't make sense that frozen beef stew containing disodium guanylate (salty, chemical flavor enhancer) would be healthier than homemade beef stew with regular salt and pepper.

Because no one wants to cook every night, there are suggestions in this chapter and in the following *Recipes* chapter for quick meals and for making enough to have leftovers.

What Are We Eating?

Most of us can easily list a number of people who are afflicted with, dying of, or have already passed due to cancer, diabetes, Parkinson's, MS, Lupus, Lou Gehrig's...the list goes on and on. Fifty years ago, we didn't have this much sickness. When I was a child, I didn't know anyone who had a fatal disease. What was different? For one thing, we didn't have fast food restaurants; no one drank cola every day, and we had very little processed food!

What about wearing glasses? Anybody who is around fifty-something knows that hardly any children wore glasses when they were in school. It was *rare*. Did you know eye doctors used to prescribe exercises to strengthen eyes rather than routinely prescribe glasses? Did you know vitamin deficiency can impact your eyesight? *(More about eyes on pages 119-120)*

Is it our air? Is it our environment? Is it stress in our fast paced lives? Does the problem lie within our food choices? Could we make a difference in our health by paying more attention to what we are eating? The answer is "All of the above." For years, we have known about prescription drugs and growth hormones that are fed to poultry and cattle. And just think about how our eating habits have changed since fast food came onto the scene.

When fast food began in the sixties, it was an occasional treat rather than a way of life. Now, everyone has seen studies on problems with fast food. While we can't blame all illnesses on food, we know the difference between healthy and unhealthy food choices. After all, we really don't know what is added to our food. We won't know for many years – until large groups of old people (us) have fatal diseases. Then someone might trace it to chemicals and additives used in our food. Watch the movie "*Supersize Me.*"

Occasionally there will be news stories about growth hormones being given to cows so ranchers can turn a faster profit. Experts say chemicals are passed to the consumer. Have you noticed that many children are bigger and taller these days than compared with 20 years ago?

Major poultry suppliers no longer give chickens large doses of antibiotics; however, many egg-laying chickens are still housed in inhumane conditions, and there is concern about the chickens' stress affecting egg quality. What to do? Watch labels, buy top grade meat from reputable sources and buy organic if possible. We must educate ourselves, make good choices (within our grocery budgets), take good vitamins, and be aware of toxins in our food.

EASY COOKING INGREDIENTS

The goal of easy cooking is to use as few ingredients as possible – but get maximum flavor! The recipes in this book do not contain unusual ingredients. Stock your pantry with the following items (plus some meat in your freezer) to prepare most of the recipes in this book. Items needed for the desserts/party foods are not included in this list.

Store brands work fine in most instances.
chicken broth: Read the labels on chicken broth. If you cannot make your own, buy organic chicken broth. Or just use water with 1 tbsp butter and 1 tbsp olive oil.
spices: garlic powder, onion powder, cumin, basil, and Italian blend
15 oz cans of diced tomatoes (plain)
tomato paste (6 oz cans)
sliced black olives (optional ingredients in several recipes)
extra-virgin olive oil

Parmesan cheese (you might want to buy the extra large "bulk" size)
Pasta – white flour is not the best choice; if you don't like whole
　　　wheat, go for organic semolina. It costs a little more, but is
　　　a denser noodle and a smaller quantity is more satisfying.
celery (great in stir fry, stew and for snacks)
lemons or bottle of lemon juice (store brand is fine)
soy sauce (low or less sodium)
flour (if you buy Self-Rising, don't ever add salt or baking powder)
cornstarch – for most recipes, you can use either cornstarch or flour
corn meal
rice
butter
cooking spray (store brand is fine – buy olive oil or canola oil)

About Spices

Contrary to what manufacturers want us to believe, spices do not lose any significant flavor when they've been on the shelf for a while. Just take the lid off and take a good whiff. Keep your spices behind cabinet doors, not exposed to light; however, light should only affect the color, not the taste. Heat will ruin your spices; do not store them in the cabinet over the stovetop or oven.

Buy name brand Italian herb blends. Off-brand or Dollar Store versions might be bitter and not contain an actual assortment of herbs. Check your labels!

Flash Freezing

Flash freezing means to freeze your small items separately so they will not stick together when placed in a large bag. This method is great for chicken (tenders, breasts, legs, and thighs), hamburgers, stir-fry meat slices, peppers (cut peppers into strips), pork chops, etc.

On an ungreased cookie sheet, lay out your items. Items should not touch. Put the cookie sheet in your freezer long enough to freeze the food. Peppers will not take as long as meat. Once items are well frozen (an hour or longer for meat), remove from cookie sheet with a sturdy spatula and put in a large freezer bag. The food will not stick together, and you can remove only what you need for your meal. If you forget and leave the cookie sheet in the freezer overnight, the food is still usable, just a little drier.

About Meat

If you have a pound of ground meat in the freezer and some pasta or rice, you can make dinner. A few other ingredients can make it special. Tomato sauce and a few spices make an Italian pasta. No tomato sauce? Make a white sauce for pasta (page 97) or hamburger stroganoff (page 95).

Buy meat when it is on sale and freeze it. For ground chuck, buy large quantities and divide it into one pound or larger packages, then freeze. 90% lean is best and you don't have to drain it. Ground meat is easy to defrost. If you don't have a microwave, put the frozen meat in a heavy pan (cast iron is best) on low heat with a half cup of water. Watch it closely, scraping off the meat as it defrosts and cooks. Cover with lid to help the heat steam and defrost meat.

Make a couple of meatloaves (see recipe) and freeze them.

If you don't want to flash-freeze your burger patties, make them and store each one individually in a sandwich baggie (so they won't stick together). Since the baggies have been used for raw meat, it probably isn't a good idea to reuse them.

Ground turkey breast is a good, low fat alternative to ground beef. Watch your labels; dark turkey meat has more fat than ground beef. Because white turkey is low fat, it <u>will</u> stick and burn if you are not careful. Ground turkey is great for spaghetti, chili, meat loaf, and other recipes that use a sauce. Turkey burgers taste fine with some extra spices, but turkey does not stick together as well as ground beef does. I do not cook turkey burgers on the grill.

Turkey is not as lumpy as ground beef and makes a smoother sauce. You can also mix half turkey and half ground beef.

If you eat pork, watch grocery sales and buy a big ham. If you don't buy hams because they are so salty, try a different brand. Hamilton or Smithfield hams are usually good. Whatever brand you buy, get a whole ham (on sale) and ask the butcher to cut it in half so you can freeze the rest. To remove excess salt, wash the ham before cooking. Buy a boneless pork loin (or roast) on sale for a budget-easy meal. With planning, you can get several meals from one roast. The *Picnic* is a fattier cut of meat. Some cooks prefer to boil a picnic before baking to remove some of the fat and excess salt.

About Poultry

Boneless, skinless chicken breast fillets or tenders (frequently on sale) are very versatile. Chicken tenders are easiest to use for a variety of recipes. Boneless, skinless thigh meat is also good; however, it does not have the density of the white meal and therefore isn't as filling (it also has a higher fat content).

Stir Fry (see Recipes) can be a great budget stretcher. Make more than you need so you will have leftovers for lunch or after school snacks – or even another dinner!

Try cutting boneless chicken breast fillets in half (cut from side) and cook them like little chicken steaks or for sandwiches.

Never defrost chicken or turkey in the microwave. It will be tough. Instead, put frozen, sealed package in cool water. Changing the water every 30 minutes will help it thaw more quickly.

Watch labels and avoid brands that are heavily salted – which usually means they keep their chicken on the shelf longer. Salt is a preservative. Also, we don't need to consume extra salt.

Thoroughly wash your chicken; wash your counters after preparing chicken, and be sure to wash your hands and knives before handling other food. If you use a cutting board, do not use it for chicken then vegetables – wash the board or use a different one.

What Is In Your Freezer?

Years ago, we had a problem with "weevils" – those little, slow-moving, hard shelled critters that get into flour, pasta, and other food items. When I found them in the Jell-O, I decided to put everything in the freezer: flour, grits, confectioner's sugar, brown sugar, rice, cake mixes, and Jell-O. After a while, all the bugs vanished, so I no longer keep all those items in the freezer. *Some people say a bay leaf will keep the critters out.*

Another freezer use – ant invasion. One summer I bought a large bag of cat food and put it in an open canister in the cabinet. Two days later, the entire canister was full of ants. I *really* didn't want to throw it away. I put the canister in the freezer, and it worked like a charm! I froze the food (and ants), then removed the canister from the freezer. The ants mysteriously disappeared, and the cats didn't seem to notice any difference in the food.

If a food item has gone bad and trash day is days away, store the offensive item in the freezer until you can dispose of it.

POTS & PANS

- **STOVETOP TO OVEN – POT with lid (Dutch Oven):** This should hold about 5 quarts. Stainless steel or cast iron is best. To prevent rust on cast iron, place in warm oven after washing, then coat lightly with oil to store.

- **9 X 13 PAN:** Great pan for sheet cakes and several recipes in the next chapter. Difficult to find in stainless steel. I do not use tomato products in aluminum because of the still-under-research connection to Alzheimer's disease. Non-stick pans are good, but throw them away if they start to flake. Glass is preferable to aluminum but much heavier. The **11x14 lasagna pan** is also handy to have, especially if you cook large amounts; try to buy stainless steel.

- **LARGE POT with lid** for cooking pasta and rice, and at least one **SAUCE PAN** with lid for veggies. Stainless steel is best. Experts say to properly cook rice, your pot should have a tight-fitting lid.

- **FRYING PAN:** Teflon is easier to clean but it doesn't brown foods as nicely as cast iron does. I prefer Teflon for frying or scrambling eggs.

- **WOK:** For Chinese food, a wok is very handy. Although you can use a large, deep frying pan, a wok is much easier to use (especially if it has a handle). The wok's high sides and round bottom make it easier to turn your food. Non-stick is preferable for a wok; it lets you use less oil. Always use non-metal utensils for stirring.

- **OTHER**: Cookie sheets, 2 round cake pans, 9x9 and 8x8 square pans, a 2 quart casserole, 1 sheet pan with sides – about 10"x 15", and a roaster (or use the lasagna pan)

- **BASIC IMPLEMENTS:** measuring cups & spoons, sharp knives, slotted spoons (serving and stirring), potato masher, flat spatula for turning, rubber spatula for scraping, tongs, can opener, grater, wire rack, and colander.

STORE BRANDS VS. NAME BRANDS

Many store brands are prepared at the same company, but different recipes are used. Most store brands are not noticeably different from brand names; however, sometimes the differences are significant. Don't stock up until you have tried the product, and keep your receipt so you can return the item if you don't like it.

MARGARINE, BUTTER, AND ZERO TRANS FAT

The butter vs. margarine controversy rages on. Researchers say even though we love the super soft, easy-to-spread kind, it is *not* good for us. The harder the margarine, the better (or less bad) it is. Hydrogenated oils (trans fat) are thought to be the main culprit. This information is true with crackers, chips and other products, not just margarine. If you use margarine, use one of the "heart smart" brands with no hydrogenated oil. Stick butter (real butter) is less expensive and has no additives; however, some sources believe it has dangerous levels of saturated fat.

OLIVE OIL

Studies have shown that olive oil is good for you, but only as a *replacement* for other oils. Using large quantities of any oil is not good for the body, but olive oil is a better choice. One Tbsp oil and one Tbsp butter is a delicious way to sauté onions or an onion/pepper mix. Most health websites suggest canola oil for high heat.

MILK

Buying organic products is more expensive, but some items matter more than others. Research shows that organic milk is a good choice. If you investigate Mad Cow Disease and see what is being fed to some of these poor creatures, you will understand the importance of organic milk.

SNACKS

Fruit and fresh veggies are the best choices, but basic snack items can include Ritz crackers (whole wheat), soda crackers, peanut butter; raisins and peanuts make a wholesome snack, raisins and almonds are even better. Prepared snacks are much more expensive than spreading peanut butter on Ritz crackers. It costs less than anything you can buy that's already prepared; it's fairly nutritious, and most kids love it.

Another quick snack is cheese nachos. Put some taco chips on a plate, sprinkle with shredded cheese, and microwave for 20 seconds. Use a glass plate or a coated paper plate so it won't stick to the plate.

Note: Although white flour products say "enriched" (adding some vitamins/minerals back in), white flour (like crackers) is not the healthiest choice. However, it is more budget friendly. If you include white flour in your diet (and most of us do), make sure you also eat fresh fruit and vegetables (raw is best) and take a good multivitamin. Cheap white bread is not a healthy choice.

MORE SNACK IDEAS

Popcorn (the new, safer microwave type) or pop your own
Cut up celery and baby carrots (or cut up carrot sticks)
Pretzels
Citrus fruit
Apples (put peanut butter on apple slices)
Make Jell-O and keep a bowl in the refrigerator

Tortilla pizzas: Buy small tortillas, a jar of pizza sauce (store brand is fine), pepperoni (if you want), and shredded cheese. Take a tortilla, spread a little sauce, add pepperoni, and sprinkle with cheese. Heat in oven at 300° just until cheese melts. Or you can use a toaster oven or heat in the microwave for about 20 seconds.

Pizza Wrap: take a small tortilla, spread on pizza sauce (optional), put several pepperonis down the middle (optional), and sprinkle with shredded cheese. Heat, remove from oven or microwave, and fold like burrito for a great snack. This is a *snack* and does not require a large amount of cheese. Sour cream is good on it too.

Read labels and be aware of items containing *high fructose corn syrup*. You will find it in many salad dressings, too.

FAVORITE KITCHEN HINTS

- Always keep your kitchen drawers closed.

- When mixing flour with liquid, you will have fewer lumps if the liquid is cold. For homemade pie crust, use ice water.

- One of my favorite utensils is the "Mini Whipper" by *Pampered Chef*™. It costs around $3. The whipper is not advertised for sauces, but it is wonderful for making gravy. I have never had lumpy gravy or sauces since getting that tool! www.pamperedchef.com

- To grease pans, keep one good-quality brush in a heavy-duty baggie next to your can of Crisco. You will have to change the baggie from time to time because the grease will seep through, but you don't have to wash a brush each time you grease a pan.

- Dip cut apples in pineapple juice to prevent browning. (Using salt water or lemon juice affects the taste.)

- If food is too salty, add thick slices of raw potato (throw potato away when finished cooking). This will help some, but it won't correct a badly over-salted dish.

- If food is a little bitter, add a bit of sugar. Add sugar in very small amounts.

- If your sauce is too sweet, add ½ tsp. white vinegar. You might need to add more, but add it a little at a time so you don't make your sauce taste like vinegar.

- Do not use celery leaves – they are bitter.

- If you need to ripen fruit, put it in a plastic or paper grocery store bag and twist tie the top. Check the progress at least once a day.

- If you lay bananas on top of a basket of apples, the bananas will ripen too fast.

- Can't find your cake tester? Use a dry spaghetti noodle to check your cake for doneness. You can also use a knife, but it makes a bigger hole.

- Put ¼ tsp. rice inside your salt shaker to keep salt from clumping in humid weather.

- For the ultimate burger, squeeze a bit of ketchup on the bottom as well as on top of the burger!

- Cut green (and colored) peppers into strips and freeze.

- Roast green or colored peppers. Line a pan (with sides) with foil. Core peppers and remove seeds. Lay peppers on side in pan and broil. Watch closely! Turn peppers to brown (almost burn) on all sides. Remove pan from oven and let cool about 10 minutes. Remove skin, cut peppers into strips and flash freeze. *See "Flash Freezing" on page 78.*

- When making a large casserole or stew, serve the plates or bowls before putting them on the table. When a large dish is on the table, it is tempting for everyone to overeat. If you want leftovers, leave the serving bowl in the kitchen.

- To microwave stale bread, wet a paper towel and wring it dry. Wrap around bread (cover completely) and microwave for 10-15 seconds.

- If you are serving a platter of sandwiches, wet paper towels and wring "dry." Spread over sandwiches until you are ready to serve. If making sandwiches the night before, cover with wrung-out paper towels, then cover with plastic wrap to refrigerate. *If you do not wring all the water out of those paper towels, you will have soggy sandwiches!*

- Don't dirty a rack to cool cookies, use paper towels. This also works for cakes!

- Dirty microwave? Heat a cup of water in microwave on high for a minute. The steam from the boiling water will soften the grime, then wipe with a sponge or paper towel. Vinegar in the water will deodorize the microwave.

- If you are always running out of milk for your coffee, make some milk "ice cubes" and keep them in a bag in the freezer. Or freeze a cup of milk. Make sure you use a container large enough for the milk to expand as it freezes.

- If the mixing bowl is sliding on your counter, place a damp cloth or damp paper towel under the bowl.

- If you are rolling something out on wax paper, wet the counter with a damp sponge or cloth so the wax paper will stick to the counter.

- Buttermilk: if your recipe calls for buttermilk, use regular milk and add one Tbsp lemon juice to one cup milk.

- To neutralize strong cooking smells, wipe the cooking area with white vinegar or simmer vinegar in a sauce pan.

- Are your plastic storage containers sticky? Make a paste of baking soda and water to scrub it. (Start with 1 Tbsp baking soda and just enough water to make it a paste consistency.)

- Natural air freshener: cut up an orange (or use orange peel) and simmer in a cup of water on the stove. At Christmas, it's nice to add some cinnamon (stick or ground), and your house will have a lovely aroma.

- If you're cooking a pie with meringue: when meringue is brown, turn off oven and leave door open to let pie cool slowly – to keep meringue from splitting.

- Is your baking powder still good? It is usually good long after the expiration date. Drop a pinch into a cup of warm water. If it fizzes, it is still good.

- Fresh air is a good deodorizer. For hard plastic (trash cans, cat box, etc.) put in bright sun for an hour or longer. For colored bedding, hang in shady area. The sun also bleaches!

- Use a wet paper towel to pick up shards of glass.

- Make stale chips or crackers crispy again by baking in oven about 10 minutes at 250°.

- Use a large piece of eggshell to pick out smaller pieces.

- Pesky fruit flies? Put cider vinegar in a small shallow dish and add a few drops of dishwashing liquid. Or put a 2 inch piece of fruit in a small baggie and close the bag leaving only a small opening. The flies will go in but they won't be able to find the way out.

- Teflon Pans: if the coating starts to peel, throw the pan away. The flakes of chemicals will be in your food.

- Nappa is a light, mild-flavored cabbage that adds color, texture, and fiber to many dishes. Excellent in stir fry, it is a nice addition to stews, a chicken & rice dish, or a vegetable medley. Romaine lettuce can also be used in the same way.

- Keep raw shrimp and chicken chunks in your freezer. When you need a quick dinner, cook some pasta, add some shrimp or chicken to the water before the pasta finishes cooking, then drain and add parmesan cheese & butter for dinner in less than ten minutes! If you like broccoli, add a handful of florets to cook with the pasta (about 3 minutes) for a well balanced meal cooked in one pot. *Cook shrimp 3-4 minutes; cook chicken 5-6 minutes or until done.*

- Fire in the grill? Milk will extinguish it quickly.

- Always protect your hands with rubber gloves when washing dishes.

- Fire in the kitchen? A wet dishtowel is a good choice because you don't have to get as close to the flames as you would to use a lid. The towel will cover most any size pan. or large area. (Never pour water on a grease fire.)

- When transporting food, always cover it with plastic wrap or foil – even if it is a plate of cookies you're giving to a friend.

COOKING BASICS – MEASUREMENTS

- Tbsp = tablespoon
  tsp = teaspoon

- 3 tsp   = 1 Tbsp   = ½ oz
  2 Tbsp   = 1/8 cup = 1 oz
  4 Tbsp   = ¼ cup   = 2 oz
  5 1/3 Tbsp   = 1/3 cup = 2 2/3 oz
  8 Tbsp   = ½ cup   = 4 oz (one stick of butter is ½ cup)
  16 Tbsp   = 1 cup   = 8 oz
  16 oz   = 2 cups   = 1 pint
  32 oz   = 4 cups   = 1 quart (qt)
  16 cups   = 4 quarts = 1 gallon

Chapter 11
Favorite Recipes
Give us each day our daily bread. Luke 11:3

About the recipes:
The recipes are a collection of foods enjoyed by my family. We hope you like them, too. For the most part, they are just basic foods that help stretch your grocery budget. There is no better way to save money (and your health) than to eat the right foods at home! *Recipes are listed in alphabetical order in the Index.*

My husband is lactose-intolerant (doesn't tolerate dairy products); therefore, few of the recipes contain dairy products, and most are low salt. Instead of milk-based gravies and sauces, mine are usually made with water or chicken broth mixed with flour or cornstarch, but using milk instead of water will make your sauce creamier and richer. Condensed soups and pre-packaged meals are not used in the recipes. Butter is a frequent ingredient, but margarine can be substituted when the recipe calls for butter.

Disclaimer: Since everyone must be so very careful these days in our sue-happy nation, I do not in any way claim that my recipes are the correct way to eat or that they are any more nutritious than any other type of food. Most of us know the right foods to eat. Whether or not we choose to eat correctly is our personal responsibility.

"REAL" RICE
Rice is a relatively inexpensive food, and there has been much debate over white vs. brown. Brown rice is recognized as a healthier choice. It has more vitamins, a higher fiber content, and is highly recommended by health experts. Lundberg, an excellent brown rice, seems readily available in the organic section of many grocery stores *(www.lundberg.com)*. Lundberg has a hearty flavor and is less "brown-tasting" than other, less expensive brown rice. This type of rice (with bran) is more costly but the grains are larger; the rice is more filling, and you use less of it.

Some recipes (like Asian foods) simply taste better with white rice. Asian countries report significantly less heart disease and obesity than the U.S; however, Asians consume a diet rich in various types of fish along with very fresh, healthy vegetables and seaweed. As fast food franchises move into Asian countries, future health trends might be interesting to follow. The McDonald's in Tokyo, Japan serves burgers but no fries – they serve white rice!

COOKING RICE: Always use twice as much water as rice. (Example: two cups of water and one cup rice.) Put measured water in pot and heat to boiling. Lid should fit tightly. Because rice boils over easily, use a bigger pot than you really need. Cover pot to bring water to boil quickly. When water is boiling, turn to low heat (simmer), then add rice. *Do not stir rice* once you put it into the water. Always cook with a lid on. The cooking instructions on the bag might say to put the rice in cold water, then cook; however, you will have fluffier rice if you bring the water to a boil first.

Brown rice takes longer to cook, about 45 minutes. Long grain white rice will take about 15 minutes. This long grain rice is well worth the extra few minutes over quick-cooking rice!

To check it, take a large spoon and gently pull back the rice to see how much water is left. If only a very small amount of water remains, put lid back on and cook for 2-3 minutes. Then turn off the heat and move pot from the burner; the rice will continue to absorb the water and be perfectly moist for serving.

CHICKEN STIR FRY

1 small onion, chopped
1 clove chopped fresh garlic or ¼ tsp. garlic powder
2 cups carrots – chop in circles, sticks, or with food chopper
3 cups broccoli florets (small pieces) OR 4 cups romaine lettuce
2-3 boneless chicken breasts (1½ lbs.) cut into bite-sized pieces
2 cups water
2 Tbsp soy sauce
1 Tbsp cornstarch
Optional: 2 cups nappa or romaine lettuce; 1 tsp grated fresh ginger, snow peas, baby corn, can of Chinese vegetables, etc. (Tear or cut nappa or romaine into manageable pieces.)

Put 2 Tbsp oil in wok or large fry pan, on medium heat. When oil is hot, add onion and garlic. *Fresh garlic burns easily; cook with onion to keep it from burning.* If using powdered garlic, sprinkle over onions. When onions are tender, add chicken and stir. Cook over medium high heat for 5 minutes. Add soy sauce and stir. Add carrots (and nappa/lettuce & ginger if using) and cover pan. If it is cooking too fast, add a bit of water and turn down heat. Cook for about 2 minutes. Add cornstarch to water and stir until smooth, then pour into pan. Add a pinch of sugar if you want. Add broccoli. With lid on pan, cook three minutes or until broccoli is tender (stick with fork) and make sure chicken is fully cooked. Serve with rice.

The great thing about Stir Fry is that you can add whatever you want. If you don't like onions or don't have one, just use other vegetables. *Stretch it* by adding baby corn or a can of Chinese vegetables, nappa (Chinese cabbage) or romaine lettuce, mushrooms, chopped celery, snow peas, or whatever you like. Fresh grated ginger root is a great flavoring. Although it looks expensive, it weighs very little and a good-sized piece will cost less than $1. Just break a section off the larger piece at the store. To use, peel a small section, then grate into your food while you are cooking. The fresh citrus flavor is wonderful, and it smells good too.

You can also stretch this dish by adding more vegetables. The idea behind Chinese cooking is more veggies, less meat. Just make sure you have a good sauce to make the rice delicious. If you want to try a different flavor, buy Hoisin Sauce at the grocery store. One Tbsp of Hoisin will make regular stir fry taste like a gourmet meal! *Hoisin and Soy Sauce are salty.*

For a budget stretcher, use Ramen noodles. Make the meal as listed above, but omit cornstarch. Measure two cups of water and add the flavor packet from the Ramen noodles, stir well. Add water to pan. My children loved it; however, a Ramen noodle package can add an extra 300 calories to your dish. Serve as is or over rice.

SEAFOOD STIR FRY

Use your choice of favorite vegetables, then add scallops and/or shrimp (peeled and de-veined). Put those in *last* because they cook quickly. If cooked too long, they will have the consistency of rubber. Shrimp and scallops should be cooked about 3 minutes. Raw shrimp will change color from gray to pink. Cook large scallops longer than bay (small) scallops.

CHINESE SOUP (for 2-3 people)

Make Chinese soup to go with your Stir Fry. Heat chicken broth (two cups broth plus ½ cup water) to low boil, add a few scallops, some shrimp (about 3 per person), one cup nappa or romaine and a few snow peas. Or use chunks of chicken or pork and add a few vegetables. Be creative and enjoy!

CRISPY NOODLES To serve crispy "soup noodles," buy won-ton wrappers and deep fry. For healthier version, brush wrapper with oil and bake 5 minutes at 350°. Not as good as fried, but crunchy! Be sure to cut wrapper into three or four strips before cooking.

FRIED RICE

4 (or more) cups COLD, cooked rice
1 - 2 cups of meat (chicken, beef, or pork) – *whatever you have; this is a "leftovers" meal. You can also make it all veggies.*
water or chicken broth as needed to moisten rice
2 Tbsp soy sauce
¼ tsp garlic powder (or one clove fresh garlic– chopped)
1 tsp onion powder (or ½ cup chopped onions)
1 cup chopped carrots
1 cup each (of what you like): beans, peas, corn, celery, etc.

The time involved is prep time. Actual cooking time is less than ten minutes. Cut your carrots and other vegetables into small pieces or use a can of Veg-All. I use fresh carrots, 3-4 stalks chopped celery, ½ can of green beans, ½ can of green peas, and ½ can of corn. Cut the green beans into smaller pieces (about ½ inch). Store remainder of vegetables for another meal or freeze to put into soup. We like onions, so I chop up a large onion. If you do not like onions (or any other veggies mentioned), just don't use them.

If you are using fresh onions, cook onions and carrots (and celery) first, at medium high heat. Add soy sauce and spices, then stir. Add chopped meat and any canned vegetables. Let meat and veggies heat for 5 minutes, then add rice. Reduce heat to medium low and let mixture warm; add a bit of water and break up the lumps of cold rice. Heats faster if covered. Do not let rice stick to the pan – and don't add too much water or you will have soup. Stir and turn until mixture is heated through, then serve.

HAMBURGER MACARONI

3 cups elbow macaroni (or other similar pasta)
1½ lbs. (or more) ground meat (or ground turkey)
two 6 oz cans tomato paste or one 12 oz can
3 cups water (24 oz)
½ tsp garlic powder
1 tsp onion powder
salt and pepper to taste

Prepare in large pot (Dutch oven is good). Brown meat while boiling water to cook macaroni according to directions (in separate pot). Drain meat, return it to pot. Add tomato paste and stir to coat meat, then add water and spices. When mixture is heated through, add cooked macaroni. Serve as stew or add more water to make it more of a soup. Serve with salad for a healthy meal.

HAMBURGER POTATO (Suitable for crock pot)

Same as above but instead of macaroni, slice 5 - 6 medium potatoes (1/4 to 1/2 inch thick slices). Add potatoes after meat & broth reach low boil. Cook on medium heat until potatoes are tender (check with fork). This is a great dish for potato lovers. It is a favorite at our house.

SPAGHETTI SAUCE (Suitable for crock pot)

Few people take time to make their own spaghetti sauce these days. I will not include a recipe for homemade because there are lots of recipes. I prefer just adding meat to organic, store-bought spaghetti sauce. The sauce is thick, and I always add some water. Here are some suggestions to spice up your meals.

We like to vary our spaghetti with mild Italian sausage, chicken with chunks of green pepper, or pork chops. Pork is better if cooked separately (fry, bake or grill) and add drippings to the sauce. For variety, use different types of pasta. Serve your sauce over angel hair pasta one night and over ziti the next night; it tastes like a different dish.

We love cottage cheese and cooked leaf spinach with our spaghetti. If it sounds odd, remember that cottage cheese can be substituted for ricotta cheese in lasagna – and a spinach mix is used for stuffing large pasta shells in several Italian dishes.

Cioppino: Buy ½ lb. cleaned shelled shrimp, ¼ lb. scallops, ½ lb. mild fish fillet (cod or tilapia), one can clams (pour clams & liquid in sauce), and mussels (optional). Cut fish fillet into bite-sized pieces. Use two jars sauce, one can diced tomatoes, and enough water to make the consistency you like. Heat sauce while pasta is cooking. Five minutes before you're ready to serve, add seafood and cook for 5-6 minutes on medium heat. Fish cooks quickly. If you're using raw shrimp, it turns pink when done.

MEATLOAF

1½ lb ground chuck or ground turkey (or half beef & half turkey)
1 cup oatmeal
½ Tbsp garlic powder
1 tsp onion powder or ½ cup chopped onions
1 egg
1 can (12 oz) tomato sauce
½ cup water
1/3 cup green peppers (optional)

Preheat oven to 325°. Put first five ingredients in large bowl and squish together to blend spices. Add tomato sauce and water and squish in with the meat mixture. Put in loaf pan (sprayed with cooking spray), spread ketchup over entire top, and cook for 1½ hours or until done. *Buy 90% ground beef to eliminate grease.*

While your hands and bowls are messy, why not make another meatloaf or two to put in the freezer? Form meatloaf into pan and freeze. Once frozen, run water on bottom of pan to release loaf from pan, then wrap loaf and return to freezer. Or prepare mixture and freeze in freezer bag; once defrosted, you can shape it into the loaf pan. Pack securely in freezer bag or aluminum foil.

You can also double the recipe and free-form your loaf in a larger pan.

MINI MEATLOAVES – great for sandwiches

Does your family like meatloaf sandwiches? While your hands are already messy from making meatloaf, you could make mini meatloaves! These are great for individual servings and sandwiches. Make the meatloaf as above, but use a shallow dish or pan (with sides) for cooking. With your hands, shape the mixture into individual serving sizes. If you know they will be used primarily for sandwiches, make them roughly the size of the bread you will be using – basically a square patty. Can be frozen before or after cooking. If you're making sandwiches to go, spread a thin layer of butter or mayonnaise on each slice of bread. That should keep most grease or ketchup from going through the bread.

BEEF STEW (Suitable for crock pot)

1+ lbs stew beef (could be less or more meat)
1/4 cup flour (optional)
¼ tsp garlic powder, ½ tsp onion powder (or onions)
2 Tbsp cooking oil *(I use olive oil and 1 Tbsp butter)*
vegetables – traditional veggies are potatoes and carrots; you can add
      onion, celery, zucchini, peas, nappa, romaine, etc.
use Dutch Oven or other heavy pan

Stew is a dish that might vary each time you make it. You can add more or less potatoes, carrots, etc. A good rule of thumb is 3-4 potatoes, 3-4 peeled carrots, 2-3 stalks of celery, two cups torn romaine – all cut in about 1 inch pieces.

If using flour, put flour in large food storage bag (cheap bags, not Zip Lock) or paper bag. Put stew beef into bag, hold it closed, and shake to lightly coat the meat with flour (this is called dredging). Put cooking oil in pot and heat to medium. Add meat. Be ready with a slotted cooking spoon to stir and brown the beef. You needn't spend a lot of time with this; just turn beef over a few times.

When beef is mostly browned, add spices and four cups water (or more, depending on how much stew you're making). Add what you like. I use ½ tsp garlic, 1 tsp onion powder (or fresh onions), and salt and pepper to taste. If you have time, simmer about two hours for maximum flavor, then add vegetables and simmer one more hour. However, you can brown the meat, then add vegetables and cook at a higher temperature until vegetables are tender. Your meat might not be quite as tender, but you will still have a good dinner. Keep stew covered while cooking or your broth will cook away.

To cook in crock pot, prepare meat with flour, but do not add oil. Add spices and vegetables plus two cups water and set to cook while you're away.

Serve with rice to stretch it.

BEEF STEW FROM THE MICROWAVE

If you have a microwave, beef stew is a good recipe when you have forgotten to take something out of the freezer for dinner. Defrost beef in the microwave. Cut up vegetables and cook in four cups water (on the stove) while meat is defrosting. Cook meat in the microwave until done, then simmer in sauce with vegetables for about thirty minutes. Overcooking stew beef results in incredibly tender, melt-in-your-mouth beef.

When you microwave the meat, you won't have the same sauce as when you have cooked it for hours in water. To thicken your broth a bit, take 2 cups cold water and stir in one Tbsp cornstarch until dissolved. Add to meat with one Tbsp butter. Cook on medium heat and stir until broth begins to thicken. If you want a thicker broth, repeat step with ½ cup water and 1 tsp cornstarch.

BEEF TIPS OVER RICE

Cook beef as in stew recipe above (brown then add water to barely cover). Dissolve 2 Tbsp flour in 2 cups of cold water, add 1 tsp onion powder, then add to meat. Cook over low heat until sauce thickens. Salt and pepper to taste. •Can also be a microwave meal. When beef is tender, put in pot with enough water to cover the beef, then follow above sauce directions. Serve with rice.

HAMBURGER STROGANOFF

1 lb ground meat (or use sliced flank steak or roast, thinly sliced)
1 Tbsp grated onion OR   ½ tsp onion powder
¼ tsp garlic powder
1 Tbsp butter – or olive oil
2 cups water with one Tbsp flour OR corn starch
½ cup sour cream
16 oz wide noodles – cook according to package directions

Brown ground meat and drain grease. While meat is in colander, put butter in pot and melt on low. Grate onion into butter and add garlic. Cook for a minute or so and put ground meat back into pot. Pour one cup water over meat. Dissolve flour in one cup cold water; stir well to remove lumps. Add to sauce and stir as it thickens. When you are almost ready to serve, add ½ cup sour cream. Reduce heat and cook five minutes. Recipe can be doubled.

CHICKEN TETRAZZINI

2-3 boneless chicken breasts (about 1½ lbs.), cut in chunks
3 cups water (can use chicken broth or milk)
2 Tbsp butter (for sauce)
 If you use chicken broth and/or milk instead of all water,
 only add one Tbsp butter
2 Tbsp oil (to cook chicken)
2 Tbsp corn starch
½ tsp garlic powder
1 Tbsp onion powder
1 lb pasta (spaghetti or any pasta)
1 small can of sliced black olives (optional)
½ cup parmesan cheese

Preheat oven to 350°. Grease (or spray) a 9 x 13 pan. Cook pasta while you are preparing sauce. In Dutch oven, brown chicken in oil. Combine cornstarch, garlic, and onion powder in cold water. Stir until smooth; add to chicken and stir as sauce thickens. Cook on medium heat. Add black olives and parmesan cheese. Drain pasta and pour into chicken mixture. Stir well. Pour pasta and chicken mixture into greased pan, cover with foil, and bake for 20 minutes. If it dries out a little, add ½ cup of water or milk and stir.

If you are in a hurry, just mix sauce with pasta and serve. This dish also freezes well. From freezer, bake for 30 to 45 minutes or until heated through (until it's a little bubbly on top).

CHICKEN & SAUSAGE STEW *(Suitable for crock pot)*
boneless, skinless chicken breasts (2 - 3 pieces)
> cut into roughly one inch pieces

1 pkg mild Italian sausage (5 pieces); cut into ½ inch pieces
4 lg or 6 medium potatoes, cut into chunks
4 or 5 large carrots cut into chunks
4 stalks celery – optional, but a great addition
small onion (cut into chunks) – optional
four cups water or chicken broth
cornstarch (use if you want a thicker broth)
In this recipe, DO NOT add any salt or spices. The sausage has all the spices you need.

In Dutch Oven, cook chicken and sausage about 20 minutes while you're getting the potatoes and carrots ready. Add 3 cups water or broth. Add potatoes and carrots to pot and cover. If using cornstarch, dissolve one Tbsp into cold water and add to broth.

Once all of the ingredients are in the pot, put lid on and turn to low heat. Cook until carrots and potatoes are tender. You might need to add more water. Celery adds great flavor.

While it is very good when done, it is even better the next day. If you need to stretch this, serve it over rice or pasta.

SAUSAGE STEW (QUICK)
1 package mild Italian sausage or Bratwurst (fresh or frozen)
4 lg or 6 medium potatoes, cut into chunks
4 or 5 large carrots cut into chunks *optional*
onion (cut into chunks) *optional*
3-4 stalks celery *optional, but a great addition*

If sausage is frozen, no need to defrost. Put sausage into Dutch Oven with a cup of water. Cover with lid and cook on medium heat. If sausage is frozen, it will take longer to cook. While sausage is cooking, cut up potatoes and other vegetables. When sausage is cooked enough to cut, remove one at a time to cut into chunks and return to pot. Then add chopped vegetables and enough water to cover the meat and vegetables. Cover with lid. After about 15 minutes, stir to mix sausage and vegetables. Cook on medium heat until vegetables are tender. If you need more sauce, add water. If you need to thicken the sauce, dissolve 1 Tbsp flour or corn starch in ½ cup cold water and stir into the broth. Cook 5 more minutes to thicken broth. Serve over rice to stretch it or serve with crusty bread.

WHITE SAUCE

1 lb. pasta (cook according to package)
4 egg yolks, beaten with fork
liquid: two cups water, chicken broth, or milk
2 Tbsp butter
¼ tsp garlic powder
1 tsp onion powder (or grate 1 Tbsp fresh onion)
½ cup cream cheese (optional)
½ cup Parmesan cheese (put in last)

   While pasta is cooking, mix other ingredients in saucepan. First, melt butter on low heat. Add liquid, then stir in beaten egg yolks. Do not let mixture get too hot, cook at simmer. Add spices and stir until sauce begins to thicken. If it gets too thick, add a small bit of water. If it is not thick enough, add 1 tsp. cornstarch. *(Always dissolve cornstarch in cold water before adding it to your sauce.)* Do not boil this sauce. Add salt to suit your taste.

   The sauce cooks quickly. If you use fettuccine pasta, it takes longer to cook than other pastas because it is thicker. When pasta is done, drain it and leave in colander until sauce is ready. Put pasta in large bowl and pour sauce over it.

VARIATIONS:

CHICKEN: Cut up 1+ pound of chicken breast into 1 inch pieces. Sauté chicken in two Tbsp butter for 10-15 minutes or until done. Add pinch of garlic powder and onion powder while cooking. When chicken is done, stir into sauce to simmer 5 minutes before pouring over pasta.

SHRIMP: Use 1 lb. fresh or thawed shrimp, shelled and de-veined. Add to sauce and cook on low heat until shrimp turns pink (3 – 5 minutes), then serve.

EASY OVEN CHICKEN OR CHOPS

chicken pieces OR pork chops
15 oz can of tomatoes
1 Tbsp basil (crushed between fingers), ½ tsp garlic powder, 1 tsp
   onion powder OR 2 tsp ground cumin for Tex/Mex flavor
2 cups long grain white rice
3½ cups water

   Grease bottom of 9x13 pan. Pour in water and rice, add ½ tsp salt and stir into rice. Place chicken or chops in water/rice. Mix spices with tomatoes and pour on top of meat. Cover tightly with aluminum foil and bake at 350° for 40 minutes or until done.

HOMEMADE CHICKEN SOUP (Suitable for crock pot)
One whole small chicken
1½ cups pasta (any type) OR 1 cup rice (uncooked) or 1 cup barley
one cup chopped carrots
½ cup chopped celery (not leaves)
½ cup chopped onion (optional)
1 clove garlic (or ¼ tsp garlic powder)
1 bay leaf
2 – 4 cups lettuce (not Iceburg) -- optional
1 inch piece of ginger root (optional)

In large pot, add chicken and water to cover it. Add garlic and bay leaf. Bring to boil, then turn to low heat and simmer for about 1½ hours or until done. Remove from heat. Take chicken out of water and put in colander to cool. Discard bay leaf and garlic (if used clove). While chicken is cooling, add carrots, celery & onions to broth. When chicken has cooled, de-bone it, removing all fat and small bones. Tear or cut meat into chunks.

Return chicken chunks to soup pot. Add ginger if using (and remove before serving). When vegetables are tender, bring soup to barely boiling and add pasta or rice. Keep at low boil to cook pasta. Soup is ready when pasta is tender or rice is done. If you do not have enough broth, add cans of chicken broth – do *not* add water.

Medical professionals have finally acknowledged that chicken soup has healing qualities. Especially if you are treating a cold, you should not remove all the fat from the broth.

QUICK SKILLET CHICKEN
chicken tenders – 2 good-sized pieces per person
one Tbsp butter & one Tbsp olive oil
1 cup prepared spaghetti sauce (depending on how many people
    you're serving, you might use more or less sauce)
Parmesan cheese

Sauté chicken tenders for about 15 minutes or until done (don't overcook). Heat spaghetti sauce in separate pan or in microwave. Position chicken pieces side by side in the pan. Pour spaghetti sauce across the middle of the chicken pieces (leaving the white ends showing). Sprinkle Parmesan cheese over the spaghetti sauce. Serve on bed of buttered pasta or serve without pasta and have a nice salad or veggies.

ROASTED CHICKEN (Suitable for crock pot)

To roast a whole chicken, rinse chicken inside and out, brush with olive oil, and place in pan. Add ½ cup water. To make herbed chicken (like the grocery store sells), sprinkle with basil, garlic powder, onion powder, and paprika. Cover with lid or foil and cook at 350° for 45 minutes. Remove cover and cook for another 20 minutes or until done and golden brown. When done, let "rest" for ten minutes before serving. A meat thermometer is helpful.

Roasted turkey legs are wonderful and easy to cook. Spray or grease your pan, put legs in pan, and *spray or grease the legs with oil* (to keep them moist), bake in oven at 325°. Do not cover. Cook for about 1½ hours until they have turned a lovely golden brown. You should turn them at least once.

Grill a quantity of thighs or leg quarters; separate into baggies for several meals. Can be frozen after cooking.

BURRITO WRAPS (Easy)

10" flour burritos
1 pound ground meat
1 tsp ground cumin, ¼ tsp garlic powder & ½ tsp onion powder
shredded cheese

Heat burritos according to directions on package (oven or microwave). In fry pan, brown meat and drain. Add cumin and ¾ cup of water. Simmer for about five minutes or until water has cooked out. Serve with warm burritos. Also good: shredded lettuce, diced tomatoes, black olives, sour cream and salsa to put in the wrap. Should make about 6 burritos when loaded with lettuce, olives, tomatoes, etc. Serve with chips and salsa.

OVEN WRAPS: Divide cooked meat between 6 burritos (do not pre-cook burritos; they will cook in the oven). Add shredded cheese and salsa. Wrap and place side by side in a greased 13x9 pan. Top with more shredded cheese and chunky salsa. Cook in preheated 300° oven for about 10 minutes or until cheese is melted.

BREAKFAST WRAPS: Wonderful! Heat burritos while you cook the scrambled eggs. Put about ½ cup of scrambled eggs in burrito and sprinkle with cheese. Add sausage, bacon or ham if you wish. Also a great dinner or late night snack!

CHICKEN BURRITOS: dice chicken and sauté in some olive oil with onions, green peppers, and/or other veggies. Spinach is also great, but squeeze out water or wrap with paper towel to dry.

BEEF POT ROAST *(Suitable for crock pot)*
beef (chuck, shoulder, or sirloin tip)
olive oil
½ tsp garlic powder
1 tsp onion powder
carrots, potatoes, onions, celery (add all or choose what you like).
Cooking time will depend on the size of your roast. For a 2-3 lb roast, cook at 325° for about 2½ to 3 hours until very tender. Cook covered with lid or foil. Always carve across the grain.

Put roast in Dutch Oven. Rub with olive oil and sprinkle with garlic powder and onion powder. Add vegetables and enough water to **almost** cover roast. Option: add fresh unbroken pole beans on top of other vegetables. They will steam while the roast cooks.

GOOD GRAVY
Ingredients: grease or drippings from any kind of meat
2 Tbsp flour or cornstarch (might need more)
water, milk, or broth

For gravy from a roast, chicken, pork chops, etc., use about 1/4 cup of drippings, grease, or broth. In a container or drinking glass, add 8 ounces (1 cup) of cold water (or milk) and 2 Tbsp flour or cornstarch. Stir until lumps are gone (or remove lumps). Pour into pan with meat drippings and stir. Turn heat to medium. Stir as it starts to thicken.

Watch closely and stir often. Add water as needed, about one Tbsp at a time. Water thins it out and if it gets too thin, you have to do the flour and water step again. Each time you add water, stir the gravy for a minute and let it heat through until you get the consistency you want. Use chicken broth or milk for richer gravy.
OPTION: Sauté chopped medium onion and 8 oz sliced mushrooms in 1 Tbsp olive oil and 1 Tbsp butter, then add 8 oz water. Thicken with cornstarch (one Tbsp) as explained above. Cook for 15 minutes (medium heat) for a healthier gravy.

PORK ROAST
No lid on pan. Grease or spray roaster
two or three stalks of celery (optional)
pork roast – with or without bone
1 tsp olive oil
medium-sized onion (optional)

Preheat oven to 325°. Put 2-3 stalks of celery in bottom of roaster, and position roast on top of celery (celery allows fat to drain to bottom of pan.) Rub roast with olive oil. Slice onion (thin or thick) and lay slices on top of roast. Do not cover. Cook 2½ hours or until meat is crispy. Pork should not be pink when you eat it. If you don't use a meat thermometer, slice in the middle or next to the bone to make sure it isn't pink. *If you don't have celery, cook roast on the bottom of the pan! This is a greasier piece of meat and it's better for you if it doesn't soak in the grease.*

USING THE REST OF YOUR ROAST

When cooking a beef or pork roast, you frequently end up with a chunk that isn't really big enough for another meal. Several quick & easy recipes follow, or refer to the Fried Rice recipe if you have some cold rice in the fridge (p. 91). *Suggestions for using the rest of your ham follow the beef section.*

HASH

Chop carrots, potatoes, onions, celery (whatever you like) and sauté with some butter in a deep frying pan or Dutch oven. Chop, dice, or slice roast (beef or pork) while veggies are cooking. You can also add peas, corn, and/or green beans. If you have any gravy or broth, add that. Otherwise, use chicken broth OR one cup water with a Tbsp of cornstarch or flour. Cook until vegetables are tender and meat is heated through. To stretch it, serve over rice.

ROAST & RICE

Cook four to six cups of rice. Chop, dice, or slice roast (beef or pork) while rice is cooking. Heat meat in the microwave or on the stove. Add the rice to the meat in small amounts until you get the rice/meat ratio you want. Salt and pepper to taste. The rice/meat may be a little dry. Add any gravy, drippings, or broth you have – or chicken broth or water. Add liquid a little at a time – you don't want soup. Do not add flour or cornstarch. Stir rice, meat, and broth together until warm, then serve.

BEEF VEGETABLE SOUP (Easy)

This is a great way to use up the rest of that leftover beef roast. Do NOT use any salt in this soup. Your salt will come from the canned vegetables and chicken broth you are using. Use some pepper, but let each individual salt their own if it's needed. If you do not have any original broth or gravy left over, add one tsp of soy sauce and one tsp Worcester sauce to the broth.

Cut beef into small pieces (think how small those pieces are in store-bought soup). Put beef in large pot, a Dutch Oven or larger. Check your pantry and see what you can put in your soup: a can of green beans, peas, corn, kidney beans, etc. Do not drain the liquid from these cans – dump the whole thing into your soup.

Beef, chicken, or vegetable broth is best; too much water will ruin the soup. Add a can of tomato sauce or diced tomatoes – if you like. Chopped carrots, celery, and potatoes add a great flavor. A Tbsp of parsley flakes and a tsp of onion powder should finish up your soup. If using bullion or "soup starters," read labels. Some are very high sodium (salt) and could make your soup too salty. Simmer for 20 minutes or more to blend flavors.

VEGETABLE BROTH

Cheap to make and great to keep in the freezer! Freeze in ice cube trays if you need small amounts to use while cooking (like Stir Fry) or freeze in larger containers for soup.

In four cups of water, simmer 1 Tbsp butter, 1 potato and 1 large carrot (cut into chunks) until soft, then mash well. You can also add Romaine lettuce and celery. Add more water if needed, but don't dilute your broth too much. Cook with a lid on. You can strain the broth before using, or you can leave the lettuce and small chunks in it. I use lettuce in many dishes, especially soups.

CALZONES (Easy ham recipe)

one can refrigerated pizza dough
pizza sauce (store brand is fine) or use tomato sauce and sprinkle
    with some Italian seasoning
1 cup ham, cut into small pieces (and/or other meats)
Any or all of: sliced black olives, very thinly sliced onion, sliced
    mushrooms, thinly sliced or minced green pepper
2 cups shredded mozzarella cheese

Preheat oven to 375°. Unroll pizza dough into rectangle. Cover HALF of dough lightly with pizza sauce up to about 1/2 inch from the edge. Add other ingredients and top with cheese. Fold the dough over the filling and use a fork to seal edges together. Prick top with fork and brush with egg white (optional). Bake for 20 minutes or until lightly browned.

SCALLOPED POTATOES WITH HAM
(Or omit ham and serve as side dish)
6 cups thinly sliced potatoes – boil until almost tender (5+ minutes)
1 to 2 cups bite-sized ham – chunks or slices
1 cup chopped onion
2 Tbsp butter
2 cups milk + 1 cup water + 4 Tbsp flour mixed well
1 tsp salt
¼ tsp white pepper or ½ tsp black pepper

Preheat oven to 350°. Sauté onion in butter. When tender, add milk/water/flour mixture, salt, and pepper. Drain potatoes. Pour half of potatoes in greased 2 qt. baking dish. Pour half of sauce over potatoes and mix ham into potatoes. Add remainder of potatoes and top with rest of sauce (stir ham into potatoes). Cover and bake for 20 minutes. Uncover and bake for 10 minutes.

I was not successful making this in the crock pot, but you might be more successful if you are an experienced crock pot cook.

MASHED POTATOES

If you buy the large brown potatoes, four should serve four people. If you use red potatoes (better for you), buy the large ones – not the small Irish potatoes. You will probably need to adjust the number of potatoes to your family's appetite.

Wash potatoes, cut a thin slice off the top and bottom, and cut off any obvious growth from the potato "eyes." Don't peel unless you feel you must! The thinner the slices, the faster it cooks. Put potato slices in pot that is deeper than the potatoes so it doesn't boil over. Bring water to a boil, then turn to medium heat. Do not use a lid; potatoes boil over quickly if covered. After about 15 minutes, use a fork to check tenderness. Check several potatoes to make sure. If a fork pierces the potatoes easily, the potatoes are soft enough to mash.

Drain potatoes and mash. (Buy a stainless steel masher; it will never rust.) The number of potatoes you use will affect the butter and milk ratios. For a smaller serving, use 1-2 Tbsp butter. Mash that in, then add 1/4 cup milk. You will probably need more milk, but add it slowly. You want creamy mashed potatoes, not soup! If you don't have milk, use chicken broth (and butter, of course). If you don't have milk or chicken broth, just serve boiled potato slices. *See variations on next page.*

VARIATIONS: *(adjust according to amount of potatoes!)*
- Add ½ cup sour cream and a small amount of milk. Sprinkle with chopped parsley or chives (optional).
- Along with milk and butter, add a cup of shredded, sharp cheddar cheese and a bit of garlic powder – a specialty in some restaurants!

SPICY ROASTED POTATOES
2 large baking potatoes; scrub & cut into ½ inch chunks (do not peel) or use several large red potatoes (3-4, depending on size)
¼ tsp garlic powder
¼ tsp salt
1 tsp paprika (for extra spicy, add ¼ tsp cayenne pepper)
1 Tbsp olive oil
Preheat oven to 450°. Stir garlic powder, salt, and paprika into olive oil. Toss potato chunks in mixture. Spray or grease large shallow pan. If you use foil, clean up is easy. Place potatoes in single layer in pan. Bake for 30 minutes until crusty brown; turn potatoes after 15 minutes. Check for doneness by sticking with fork.

ROASTED VEGETABLES: Add whatever you like: chunks
of potatoes, carrots, peppers, squash, onion, broccoli, etc. and toss in oil. Omit spices if you want. Bake as above.

SWEET POTATOES — *Such a healthy, versatile vegetable!*
BAKE*:* scrub potatoes, dry, then coat with some oil. Always pierce raw potatoes with a fork. Place in 400° preheated oven for 45 minutes (or until done). If the potatoes are extra large, cut them in half lengthwise, oil the cut side, and place cut side down on aluminum foil-covered baking sheet with sides.
BOIL*:* peel potatoes and slice. Put in pot and cover with water. Bring water to boil, then reduce heat to medium. Cook for about 15 minutes, then test for tenderness. Drain and mash. Add butter if you want. Don't overcook – it makes them too watery.
SAUTE*:* wash potatoes and slice thin. Heat 1Tbsp oil (or use cooking spray) on medium heat in fry pan. Add potato slices but only one layer at a time (don't pile all slices in). Cook for about 4 minutes or until tender. Serve quickly or cover with foil. This dish loses heat rapidly after cooking.
Raw sweet potatoes are a very healthy choice. Grate into salad!

BEST-EVER CORNBREAD
Preheat oven to 450°.

See mixing directions below. Add ½ cup sugar to batter and cook according to directions on the cornmeal bag. For best results, use a 10" iron skillet. Grease skillet with Crisco and place in oven for 15+ minutes. The batter should sizzle as you pour it in.

To mix: first, beat the egg. Then add milk, oil, and sugar (if you want sugar). Stir that together, THEN add the two cups of cornmeal.

All my life, I had eaten "normal" (Southern) cornbread. When I married my husband, he asked me to put sugar in it (like his mom did). It was wonderful. Leftovers make a great breakfast food–just pop in a toaster oven then top with butter.

VEGETABLES
- Change the taste of any canned vegetable by draining the liquid and simmering in chicken broth, vegetable broth, or water with a teaspoon of butter OR olive oil. You can also add a dash of onion powder and/or garlic powder. Your family will think they are eating gourmet veggies!

- Corn on the Cob: ***To Boil****:* remove shucks (green leaves) and silk (strings). Put in boiling water for 20+ minutes. Corn is done when fork can easily pierce kernels.
To Grill*:* remove silk but not shucks. Smooth shucks to mostly cover corn, then place on grill for 30-45 minutes (depending on how hot the grill is). Turn several times and don't let shucks catch fire! Corn is done when fork can easily pierce kernels.

- Cook 3-4 cups fresh broccoli florets (flor-ays). When tender, drain liquid and add Tbsp butter. Put lid on so butter will melt quickly. When butter is melted, stir to coat florets. Serve and top with sprinkling of any type grated cheese.

- Take a 16 oz bag of dried white beans and prepare according to package. When close to tender, add a frozen box (16 oz) of chopped collard greens or leaf spinach. Add 1 tsp olive oil or butter and some onion powder or grated onion. It's a great combination of flavors and a very healthy choice. *Optional:* add ham, turkey ham, or turkey bacon.

- Dried beans are good for you and are budget friendly. Cook according to the package, but it's best to let the beans soak overnight in water (rinse beans first). Throw out the soaking water and fill with fresh water for cooking. Put one tsp olive oil or butter in the beans while cooking and add salt and pepper. •For field peas or black-eyed peas, add a bit of garlic powder, onion powder or fresh diced onion, and/or green pepper. •Black beans, red beans, and garbanzo beans are delicious cold with oil & vinegar (red wine vinegar is good). Make a cold bean salad with fresh diced onion, tomatoes, and peppers or add beans to a tossed salad.

- Best Macaroni & Cheese – buy a large box of Mueller™ elbow macaroni and make the *Baked Macaroni & Cheese* recipe on the back of the box. Use sharp cheddar cheese. Double the recipe and use a 9x13 pan or large casserole dish. Also great when made with penne pasta.

- Want "fancy" baked beans but not the high price? Take a can of the cheap store brand pork 'n' beans and add one Tbsp ketchup or BBQ sauce, ½ tsp plain pancake syrup, and ¼ tsp onion powder. Simmer for five minutes.

EGGS – Not Just For Breakfast!
To Scramble: Break eggs in dish and add 1 Tbsp water per egg. Beat with fork, then add to greased (butter or cooking spray) frying pan on medium heat. Don't forget that breakfast foods can also be a good, quick, light dinner! *See page 99 for Breakfast Wraps.*

Fried Eggs: To keep from breaking eggs, crack egg onto a saucer then gently slide into warmed, greased frying pan.

Hard Boiled (and Deviled) Eggs: Some people like to start with cold water and heat to a boil. Others boil water first, then add eggs gently with a slotted spoon. Although it seems more eggs crack with the boil water first method, it is supposed to make them easier to peel. Either way, water should cover eggs. Old or spoiled eggs float.

Once water reaches a boil, set timer for 15 minutes. Lower heat to a gentle boil. After 15 minutes, remove pan from stove, pour out hot water and fill pan with cold water so eggs can cool.

Deviled Eggs:
To peel eggs, gently crack the entire shell (rap on counter) before you start peeling. Rinse after peeling, then cut eggs in half lengthwise and put yolks in separate bowl (or zip bag). Mash yolks well with fork (or mash the bag), then add enough mayonnaise (in small amounts) to make it creamy. I like to use ½ sour cream and ½ mayonnaise. Depending on how many eggs you cook, add a pinch of ground mustard (a pinch is a very small amount). Add ¼ tsp ground mustard if making a dozen eggs or more and mix well. Add a pinch of salt if necessary. When well mixed, use a spoon or pastry tool to put egg mixture back into sliced egg whites. If you're using a zip bag, cut off bottom corner and squeeze mixture into eggs, then throw bag away for a quick clean up!

BACON – *Bake it!*

Like bacon (or turkey bacon) but don't like the mess? Use a large, flat pan with sides and cover with foil. Lay out slices of bacon and cook in preheated 350° oven for 15 minutes or until done.

SALMON CROQUETTES
one can quality salmon including liquid
1 large egg
1 tsp onion powder (or 1 Tbsp grated onion)
1 tsp lemon juice (optional)
1/4 cup cornmeal
1/4 cup flour
2 Tbsp diced green pepper (optional)
Stir until well mixed. Batter will be loose. Put 2 Tbsp oil in frying pan or use cooking spray. Heat pan on high. Make patties or drop large spoonfuls of batter in hot pan. If patties are about 3"x3", you should get 8 patties. Watch pan closely. Cook for about 3 minutes on high, then flip to cook on other side. Don't let them dry out! Can serve with rice or make gravy and serve over toast.

BISQUICK RECIPES
With Bisquick, you can make pancakes, waffles, biscuits, and more. Visit **www.bettycrocker.com**. The Bisquick site is **www.bisquick.com**. Try the cheese-garlic biscuits; they are usually listed on the box. Or use a cookbook and find made-from-scratch recipes that are great and cheaper than buying a prepared product. More….

Biscuit Bread: Grease a round cake pan or pie plate and follow directions on the Bisquick box to make biscuits. Use rubber spatula to scrape all the dough into the pan. Preheat oven to 450°. Cook for ten minutes or until golden brown. Cut in pie-shaped wedges and serve with butter and jelly.

PARTY FOODS & MORE

BEST EVER ONION DIP
This recipe is on the back of the Lipton's Onion Soup package. It always gets rave reviews!
One package Lipton's Onion Soup Mix
One 16 oz container of name brand sour cream
Mix well, can be served immediately. Tastes best if it sits for a few hours (so flavors can blend) before serving.
Or make your own: 16 oz. of sour cream, add ½ tsp garlic, 1½ tsp onion powder, and 1 Tbsp minced dry onions. Mix well (see above). Add dried or fresh chopped parsley if desired.

TACO SALAD TO GO
This is a great party snack or a fun dinner. You will need:
large platter (round works well)
15 oz can of refried beans
one 8 oz container of sour cream (name brand preferred)
Tastes better if you do not use reduced fat or fat free.
taco seasoning packet OR add one Tbsp cumin to sour cream;
mix this with the sour cream as your first step
shredded cheese – 1 - 2 cups (depends on how much cheese you want to use)
Add any or all of the following (whatever you like on taco salad):
2 cups lettuce - coarsely chopped in small pieces (Romaine is best)
salsa - chunky or plain
sliced black olives - drained (small can)
tomato - small pieces
black beans
On large platter, spread out a thin layer of beans. On top of beans, spread sour cream mixture. Sprinkle with shredded cheese.
From here, add whatever you like. I generally add the lettuce, then drop small globs of chunky salsa, and top with a sprinkling of black olives. Serve with taco chips.

CHOCOLATE CHIP CAKE
Preheat oven to 350°
Bundt pan – greased and floured
One yellow Duncan Hines cake mix
1 pint sour cream
1 large package instant Jell-O chocolate pudding (store brand okay)
four eggs (room temperature)
½ cup vegetable oil
12 oz package of semi-sweet chocolate chips (store brand is okay)

Put first five ingredients in mixing bowl. Blend until everything is moist, then increase speed and beat for two minutes. Then, stir the chocolate chips into the batter (a wooden spoon works well). Pour into pan. Bake for 40 minutes and test. Watch closely so cake doesn't get too done. Cool on rack or stove eye for 20 minutes, then gently remove from pan to serving plate. To make it a little fancier, put some powdered sugar in a sifter and lightly sprinkle over cake. When taking the cake to a party, it is best to pre-slice it. This cake is always a big hit!

STRAWBERRY ICE CREAM CAKE
mixing bowl – this will be frozen: metal is best; hard plastic is okay.
    Can use heavy glass mixing bowl.
one angel food cake
one container frozen strawberries with juice (the cheap
    kind that has a lot of juice)
half gallon vanilla ice cream (cheapest is fine)
fresh strawberries for garnish (if you want)

Make sure frozen strawberries are defrosted. Take out ice cream to soften. In mixing bowl, tear the angel food cake into little pieces (one inch or smaller) and put pieces into bowl. If your child wants to help in the kitchen, this is a great kid project.

Once the cake is torn into pieces, add the defrosted strawberries and juice. Stir to mix well with the cake pieces. Add softened ice cream. You will probably use more than half the half gallon.

Stir the ice cream into the cake and strawberry mixture. Mix together well. It might be necessary to mix with your hand to get everything blended. You can decide how much ice cream you need. When finished mixing, use a spatula or spoon to smooth out the top because it will become the bottom when removed from the bowl. More….

Put cake in freezer for at least one hour or until frozen solid. If you are freezing for a longer period of time, put a good quality plastic wrap over it to prevent freezer burn.

To serve, remove cake from freezer about 20 minutes prior to serving. Place mixing bowl (rounded side up) on serving plate. Within 10-15 minutes, the cake will be loose enough for you to remove the bowl – or run bottom of bowl under very warm water for a few seconds. Garnish with sliced, fresh strawberries if you wish. Use large knife to cut the frozen cake.

STRAWBERRY SHORTCAKE
This is delicious!

one small pound-cake loaf (or make your own)
1 large box of instant vanilla pudding (store brand)
3 cups milk (to make pudding)
1 small container whipped topping (store brand)
1-2 cheapest containers of frozen strawberries - defrosted
Use a large bowl – maybe about the size of a standard mixing bowl;
*   a decorative glass bowl or pedestal bowl really shows this off!*

Strawberry juice is important for this recipe. Buy the cheap frozen strawberries that come with a lot of juice. Set aside two Tbsp of juice to use on final layer (top of dessert).

Prepare instant pudding. Cut pound cake into thin slices (about ¼ inch). In serving bowl, put a few tablespoons of pudding in the bottom. Place several slices of pound cake to cover bottom of bowl. Spoon some pudding over cake. Drizzle with 1-2 Tbsp. strawberry juice/slices. Spread thin layer of whipped topping. Place next layer of cake slices and repeat with pudding, strawberries/juice and whipped topping until you run out of ingredients. It is important for each layer to have all of the ingredients.

BE SURE to have enough ingredients (including whipped topping) left for the top layer of the dessert. Drizzle remaining juice over the top. This might be hard to explain but, for extra pizzazz, drag a plain table knife from the center to the outer edge, through the juice, several times. Just barely put the knife edge into the whipped topping and pull gently to outer edge. It will make a lovely design. In the center, put a few strawberry chunks or a large fresh strawberry with a pretty green top for the perfect finishing touch.

APPLE CRANBERRY PIE

Preheat oven to 375°
Buy a package of 2 deep dish 9" pie crusts (name brand is best)
    or make your own crust
6 cups thinly sliced tart apples (like Granny Smith)
1 cup chopped cranberries (measure 1 cup after they're chopped)
1 tsp cinnamon
½ tsp allspice
3 Tbsp flour
¾ cup granulated sugar

       Combine dry ingredients in large bowl and stir until well blended. Add apples and cranberries and stir until all pieces are coated. Put into pie crust. Mixture will be taller than crust but will cook down as the apples soften. If using purchased crusts, gently remove second crust from pan and cover pie. Crimp edges together with fork or fingers. Don't worry if the top tears or isn't smooth. Your pie should have some slits in the top – or poke several times with a fork. Sprinkle lightly with sugar. Cover edges of pie with thin pieces of aluminum foil and place pie on cookie sheet. Bake at 375° for 25 minutes, then remove foil. Reduce oven to 350° and bake an additional 30 minutes or until crust is golden brown.

BROWNIES

Brownies are always a crowd pleaser – and so easy to make. Keep mixes on hand for unexpected guests or a hungry family!

       Buy a mix that has directions for "cake like" brownies. The 9x13 pans work well for this, and you get a lot more brownies than when you use a smaller sized pan.

       Make according to package directions. While mixing, add ½ tsp of vanilla flavoring. Then add 6 oz chocolate chips and stir. You can also use peanut butter chips or white chocolate chips or chunks. Use a spatula to scrape batter into pan. Sprinkle nuts on top if you like. Bake as package directs.

       VARIATION: Do not use chocolate chips – use Hershey kisses. Prepare the cake-like brownies as directed on package and bake. When you take them out of the oven, take a dull knife and lightly outline where your cut lines will be. Then, unwrap a Hershey kiss and push it (pointed side down) into the brownie. The heat from the brownies will melt it just enough to be extra yummy.

       For easy cutting, cut brownies with a plastic knife.

CHOCOLATE CHIP MUFFINS
2 cups Bisquick (reduced fat or regular)
2/3 cup milk
1/3 cup sugar
3 Tbsp vegetable oil
one egg
½ cup semi-sweet chocolate chips
 Preheat oven to 400°. Put 12 cupcake papers in muffin tins (or grease muffin tins). Beat egg slightly then add remaining ingredients. Stir together (don't over-stir; it doesn't need to be smooth). Divide batter among the 12 muffins. Bake for 13 - 18 minutes. Check after 13 minutes – if golden brown, remove from oven.

SPICED NUTS
4 cups pecan halves (one pound)
one egg white, lightly beaten
1 Tbsp water
3/4 cup sugar
½ cup brown sugar (loose, not packed)
1 Tbsp cinnamon
1 tsp salt
½ tsp grated cloves
¼ tsp cayenne pepper (optional)
 Preheat oven to 300°. Mix dry ingredients together in small bowl. In larger bowl, beat egg white and water together. Add pecans and stir gently to coat thoroughly. Add dry ingredients and stir. Spread on ungreased baking sheet with sides. Bake 45 minutes; turn at least once. Spread on wax paper to cool. Do not use aluminum foil.

 If you're feeling adventurous, add a half can of Coca-Cola to your mix. Clean-up is tougher because it bakes onto your pan, but the glazed nuts are great! Do not use aluminum foil; nuts will stick.

SWEET PARTY MIX *(Kids love it!)*
9 cups Rice Chex cereal (or store brand)
1 cup chocolate chips
½ cup peanut butter
½ stick butter
1 tsp vanilla flavoring
½ cup powdered sugar (hold out for last step)

In microwave, melt chocolate chips, peanut butter, and butter. Stir in vanilla. Put Rice Chex in oversized bowl. Drop chocolate mixture on Rice Chex and stir to coat. Divide powdered sugar into two separate large bags (Zip-Loc type bags work best). Place Chex mixture into bags and shake to coat.

PARTY SANDWICHES
wheat bread – flat top sandwich loaves
   (1 loaf = approximately 48 sandwich quarters)
     It is best to cut crust off <u>before</u> using the spread and to slice sandwiches in quarters (cut diagonally) <u>after</u> using the spread. Use a large, serrated knife (bread knife) or an electric knife to cut the sandwiches. *To keep sandwiches fresh, see hint on page 85.*
     Recipes are generalized because the ingredients needed will vary according to the size can of tuna or chicken used. Add ingredients in small amounts. Too much mayonnaise will ruin the recipe!

PIMENTO CHEESE SPREAD:
1 large container pimento cheese
Put pimento cheese in large bowl and add the following:
   one cup grated sharp cheddar cheese (medium cheddar is okay)
   large 'dollop" of mayonnaise (about ¼ cup)
   ¼ tsp Worcestershire Sauce (shake well before using)
Mix items together well and spread thinly on bread.

CHICKEN SALAD SPREAD:
   large can of chunk chicken
   ranch dressing
   mayonnaise
Put chicken in bowl and stir well with fork to break apart clumps. Add one Tbsp Ranch Dressing and stir. Add mayonnaise in small amounts until you get the consistency you want. Add a sprinkle of onion powder and garlic powder. Add ¼ tsp celery seeds or finely chopped celery for more flavor. Mix well, spread thinly on bread.

TUNA SALAD SPREAD:
   several cans of good quality tuna packed in water
   mayonnaise
   onion powder, garlic powder, ½ tsp celery seeds
   1 tsp lemon juice (optional)
Mix until smooth and well blended. Spread thinly on bread.

WHITE CHOCOLATE POPCORN

two bags microwave popcorn or equivalent amount of freshly
    popped popcorn
one 12 oz package of white chocolate chips

Cook two bags microwave popcorn (use good quality pop-corn) or equivalent amount of fresh popped corn. Put cooked popcorn into extra large bowl (you need room to stir). While second bag of popcorn is cooking, boil water for the chocolate. This works best when the popcorn is still a bit warm.

Melt 12oz of white chocolate chips in double boiler (bottom pan holds water, top pan holds food). DO NOT melt this in a regular pan or you will ruin the chocolate. You can do this in the microwave if you watch it closely. (I am not a good microwave cook!)

As soon as chocolate is melted, pour over popcorn and mix gently with large, long-handled spoon to coat popcorn as much as possible. *If you let chocolate cook too long and it starts to get too thick, add a bit of oil – never add milk to white chocolate.*

This is incredibly good and perfect for gifts! It keeps well for about a month.

SNOW ICE CREAM

Snow is needed for this recipe! In Georgia, we're lucky if we have this treat once a year.

You will have to judge how much of the ingredients you need, but a basic rule of thumb would be:

one large raw egg
3/4 cup sugar
1 tsp. vanilla flavoring
¼ - ½ cup milk
one large mixing bowl of fresh, powdery snow

Beat egg with fork, then add sugar, milk, and vanilla – and stir well. Add snow about two cups at a time. It will melt into the liquid ingredients quickly. Depending upon how much snow you have used, you might need to add more sugar – or a little more milk if it is too dry. This does not freeze well – it becomes rock hard, but the kids still love it.

NOTE: This calls for a raw egg. Always wash your eggs (and hands) in case there is salmonella on the shell. Use this recipe at your own risk. I can only say we've eaten this all my life. Organic eggs might be a safer choice – I prefer to use them anyway.

SWEET ICED TEA

Southerners are picky about iced tea. This is my recipe for one gallon of tea. (This is <u>not</u> the old-fashioned, overly sweet, syrupy tea.)

> Four regular or decaffeinated tea bags (family size)
> > store brand works just fine
> ¾ cup sugar – or to taste
> Gallon container

Begin with cold water in tea kettle (or sauce pan with lid). When water boils, remove kettle from heat and put tea bags in water. Kettle must have a top and a "stopper" on the spout. In other words, a bit of steam will escape, but you want to keep all the flavor inside. If you use a saucepan, cover tightly with a lid. Let tea "steep" (sit) for at least 30 minutes; an hour or longer is better.

Do not pour hot tea into a glass container. If you preheat the container (with hot water), it should work but it might break. Use a plastic container. If you want to use a fancy pitcher for serving, pour your tea into a glass pitcher after you have added cold water.

Put 3/4 cup sugar in bottom of plastic gallon pitcher. Pour hot tea into pitcher. Stir well to make sure the sugar is dissolved before you add cold water. Add water but leave room for stirring. Do not fill pitcher to the brim. Watch the color of your tea. You want it to stay a darker color. If it starts looking light, you have added too much water and ruined the real taste. Taste it to see if it is sweet enough for your liking. If you need to add sugar, it is easier to dissolve at this point – before the tea is refrigerated.

Serve your delicious, home-brewed tea with fresh cut lemon or lime wedges. Some people like to use fresh mint.

PARTY PUNCH

One 2-liter regular red Hawaiian Punch
One large can of pineapple juice
Two 2-liter bottles of lemon-lime soda (Squirt, Sprite, 7-Up, etc.)

This is a great blend of flavors and a wonderfully refreshing punch. It will also stain.

SHERBET PUNCH

Half gallon of any type sherbet; use scoop to put in bowl
Two 2-liter bottles of lemon-lime soda (Squirt, Sprite, 7-Up, etc.)

Put sherbet in punch bowl and allow to soften. Add soda and gently stir 2-3 times.

Make an Ice Ring for your Punch Bowl

If you don't have a round ring pan (like for jello molds), use a bundt pan and pour enough punch in it to fill the pan half full. You can put slices of lemons, limes, oranges, and/or food-safe leaves (like mint, parsley or pansies) into the pan. As the punch freezes, the slices and leaves will float to the top. If you want the shaped part of the bundt pan to show, push the fruit slices to the bottom of the pan when the punch begins to get slushy – before it freezes solid.

Once frozen, run hot water on the bottom of the pan for about 15 seconds, and the ice ring will release easily from the metal pan. Add gently to your punch bowl.

LEMONADE – Quick & Easy

Who has time to squeeze all those lemons? But it's easy to have "homemade lemonade" at a fraction of the cost. You will need:
   one gallon pitcher
   two packages of Kool-Aid Lemonade (or similar brand)
      Buy the plain kind (without sugar)
   two cups sugar
   one lemon – cut in half. Half will be squeezed into lemonade; the
      other half will be sliced as "rounds" instead of wedges
      for decoration

Empty two Kool-Aid packs into pitcher. Add sugar and fill pitcher about halfway with cold water. Stir until sugar is completely dissolved. Squeeze one half lemon into pitcher. Fill pitcher the rest of the way. Thinly slice remaining half lemon into circles (rounds) and float on top of lemonade for decoration or cut one side about ½ inch and set on edge of glass.

For picnics or outdoor events, it is handy to use a recycled milk jug with a screw-on lid to carry lemonade.

Chapter Twelve
Health Matters
A merry heart doeth good like medicine. Proverbs 17:22

*The information offered in this chapter has not been evaluated by
the Food & Drug Administration and should not be used to diagnose, treat,
cure, or prevent any disease. Please consult your doctor regarding any
symptoms you have.*

I Can't Afford to Eat Healthy

It is true. Eating healthy is more expensive. Isn't it a shame
that it's cheaper to eat the *wrong* foods? If you are trying to feed
your family healthy meals, it might cost more money for groceries.
But look at the other side – if your family is overweight or sick much
of the time, could the right foods improve their health? Reduce
medical bills? Can you afford NOT to eat healthy – or at least
health*ier*?

If money is a major factor in your grocery shopping, try to
split the difference: have a healthy meal every *other* night. If your
child doesn't like vegetables, help her learn to like salad. Put tiny
pieces of carrots and green beans in spaghetti sauce. Get creative!

Prepared bags of salad are expensive and might be rinsed in
chemical preservatives. Get more for your money by buying a head
of Romaine lettuce. Wash it, then tear into bite-sized pieces (do not
cut with a metal knife); a plastic knife will keep lettuce from
"rusting." Put all of your pieces into a large, re-sealable baggie.
Remove as much air from the bag as possible.

Romaine and other green lettuces are more expensive, but
did you rabbits should not eat Iceberg lettuce? It can give them
diarrhea, which can kill them. If it isn't good for an animal….
Iceberg lettuce has little nutritional value. Dark green lettuce has
nutritional value as well as good fiber. Also, you have probably
noticed that fast food restaurants are finally acknowledging the
difference in lettuces. For "healthy choices," restaurants offer
Romaine. They don't say if their lettuce is rinsed in preservatives.

Portable Salad Bar

To enhance your salad experience, buy several dressings (or
use oil & vinegar). Then, make a "portable salad bar." Buy a large,
square, plastic container. Next, buy small square containers that fit

inside the big one. Put it together at the store so you will know everything fits. Put a lid on the big container, not the small ones. *You can buy round containers, but the square ones usually fit better in the refrigerator.*

The small containers hold your salad bar: black beans, chick peas, grated cheese, cucumber (keeps longer if seeds are removed), black olives, etc. The list is endless: beets, chopped green pepper, grated sweet potato, chopped tomatoes, chopped boiled eggs (eggs don't last very long), and so on. You can add broccoli, green pepper, carrots, and grape tomatoes (foods that don't spoil as quickly) to your bag of lettuce.

Once you have your portable salad bar, it is easy to make a beautiful and filling salad. Put your lettuce in a bowl, get out your portable salad bar and add whatever appeals to you, add dressing and you're ready to eat! Add meat for a wonderful chef salad.

What You Drink Matters!

If you are serious about losing weight, STOP drinking colas (including diet colas) and sweet tea. Try it for two weeks. Or, if you don't feel you can stop totally, cut down A LOT. Go from one a day to one every other day, then go to one soda/tea every three or four days, then once a week.

A word about soft drinks: although still the subject of research, there is concern that properties found in both regular cola and diet cola have an affect on the satiety mechanism of the brain. In other words, when you drink cola (diet or regular), your brain can no longer tell you when you are full and to stop eating.

Regarding diet soft drinks, there is a lot of negative information about them. When I was pregnant, my doctor said, "Do not use any products with artificial sweeteners." Aspartame can cause miscarriage and birth defects. If you talk to knowledgeable folks at a vitamin or herb shop, they will tell you how the chemicals in artificial sugars can affect you negatively in a number of ways. Check out this website on aspartame: www.dorway.com.

When my triglycerides and cholesterol numbers were high, I chose (under a doctor's care) a trial period of drinking cranberry/grape juice. Cranberry juice is good for your urinary tract (and helps with kidney problems); grape juice is a detoxifier. For three months, I drank 3 oz. of cran/grape juice every day. I made no big changes in my diet, but I did not eat fried foods or fast food, and I limited sweets. After the three months, my triglycerides and cholesterol numbers had improved significantly. The doctor no longer suggested using chemicals (prescriptions) to fix the problem.

READ THE LABEL. When you buy juice, buy the natural, 100% juice – not the ones that list sugar in the ingredients. Sucrose, fructose, and high fructose corn syrup are sugar. The pure juice will be a little more expensive than the sugar-filled brands. But, as a smart shopper, you know the first ingredient listed is mostly what you get. Just as flour is the first ingredient in breads or cake mixes, if water and high fructose corn syrup are the first ingredients in a drink, you are drinking mostly sugar. You get what you pay for.

On the label of the 100% juices (Nutritional Facts Chart), you will notice there are approximately 40 grams of sugar. This is *natural* sugar that is produced within the grape, not the same as high fructose corn syrup.

For persistent yeast or fungal infections, you might have a larger problem with Candida. Yeast feeds on sugar, whether it is a candy bar or an apple. Check online for more information and with a doctor who acknowledges this can be a problem.

Water, Water Everywhere

Water is vital to health. Your body needs it. According to colon experts, everyone should try to drink 7 – 8 tall glasses of water per day. That is a lot of water, but if you strive for a goal and fall short, it is better than not trying! Water is also a cleanser, and it will help you lose weight if you drink water instead of eating a snack – especially if you are replacing sodas. If you get tired of plain water, add lemon or lime juice or try flavored waters. Sometimes our bodies need water instead of food. A glass of water can relieve false hunger pains.

Try starting each day with a large glass of water. After sleeping 6 - 8 hours, we are in a state of dehydration and should drink water before consuming our morning caffeine fix. Coffee and tea are diuretics. Unless we drink water, we are starting our day in a totally dehydrated state.

Green Leafy Vegetables are Important

Kale, broccoli, cauliflower, Swiss chard, turnip greens, bok choy, collards, spinach, cabbage, and brussel sprouts are known to be a relatively inexpensive and important source for many nutrients needed by our bodies. Studies on these vegetables have shown they can reduce the risk of cancer and heart disease, are low in fat, high in fiber, and are rich in folic acid, potassium, magnesium, and vitamin C. They are also a good source of iron, calcium and beta-carotine (which is converted by the body into vitamin A). Vitamin A is important for improving the immune system. *Swiss chard and spinach are not the best sources for calcium.*

Greens have a high level of vitamin K, essential for strong bones. According to one study, the risk of hip fracture in middle-aged women was decreased 45% when they ate one or more servings per day of leafy green vegetables.

Another study showed eating 3+ servings of green leafy vegetables each week reduced the risk of stomach cancer, the world's fourth most reported cancer. Cabbage, broccoli, brussel sprouts, and cauliflower are reported to protect against colon cancer.

Lutein and zeaxanthin (carotenoids found in greens) protect against cataracts and macular degeneration, an age-related blindness and major problem for America's elderly. Don't wait until you are older and have a problem, eat the right foods now to protect yourself.

If you cannot eat at least three servings of greens per week, you should be taking vitamins to replace some of what you are missing. Whole food vitamins from a natural foods store are said to be the best choice. However, it is better for you and less expensive to eat the correct foods. Fresh is best; frozen is almost as good.

Eyesight and Age

Once we reach the age of forty or so, our eyesight starts to change. Being nearsighted (needing glasses for distance), mine is the reverse problem. To read or see anything up close, I must remove my glasses – because I have chosen not to wear bifocals.

Suddenly, my vision was worsening. It was most noticeable at the computer and piano. Wearing a pair of reading glasses on top of my regular glasses was very frustrating.

Probably because I was not consuming enough green leafy vegetables at that time, I sought help from vitamins. Specifically for eyes, there is a name brand, Ocuvite. I chose to purchase the less expensive Wal-Mart brand, "Equate." It contains the same ingredients as the expensive brand, but there are two types. Be sure to buy the one with the most Lutein in it. *You can buy Lutein by itself, but it seems to work better with the right combination of other vitamins.* For two weeks, I took two pills each day, then one pill each day. After the first week, I could already tell a difference. I can now work at the computer and play the piano without glasses.

A Calcium Story

About a year after the birth of my first child, I developed a pain in my right heel. I bought new expensive sneakers, thinking that the cheaper ones were the culprit. That wasn't it. I took products for pain, but nothing helped. Before going to a doctor, I decided to call an old friend who was knowledgeable about vitamins and minerals. She specified *a quality brand of calcium with magnesium and zinc*. On the second day of taking the supplement, the pain had lessened considerably. By the third day, I was pain free.

Several months later, a friend told me about a terrible pain in her heel. Her child was about six months old. I told her what had worked for me, and she called back a few days later to report the same success that I had.

At a Saturday afternoon party, one of the moms said she was scheduled for exploratory surgery on her heel the following Monday. Her baby was a few months old. I told her about my calcium experience. Weeks later, she saw me in the grocery store and was excited to tell me about her heel. After leaving the party, she bought the calcium/magnesium/zinc on her way home. By Sunday night, her pain was almost gone, so she canceled the Monday surgery. She continued taking the calcium and had no more pain. Her doctor was mystified, but her problem was cured.

A calcium deficiency can affect your teeth. Tooth sensitivity or an increase in cavities could be the result of low calcium levels rather than a need for special toothpaste.

Also, calcium is the body's natural way of handling pain. I once had a very painful area in my upper right arm. I finally went to the doctor; an x-ray that showed nothing, and physical therapy was prescribed. The therapy was too expensive and, I don't remember the reason now, but I decided to try calcium. The pain was gone the next day. Calcium also can be effective for RLS (restless leg syndrome).

Constipation may occur when you first take calcium. This is easily fixed with green leafy vegetables and other fiber.

Magnesium is very important to take with calcium (for heart health), and vitamin D is important for your body to absorb calcium. The latest surprising widespread deficiency is vitamin D. Although the sun is a great source, experts can't seem to agree on how much sun a person needs. Of course, it is best for your doctor to do a blood test to determine if you have a deficiency (or other problems). Self-diagnosis doesn't always work!

Doctoring On a Budget

While there is no replacement for a good diet, most of us do not eat right and would benefit from a good daily multivitamin. Many people consider themselves basically healthy but seem to get sick too often. A healthy immune system allows us to fight off illness. There are several immune-boosting products on the market, one of which is acidophilus (which you might know from watching yogurt commercials). If you are frequently ill, work on boosting your immune system.

To stock your medicine cabinet: Band-Aids, Neosporin, Acetaminophen (Tylenol), Ibuprofen, Benadryl, and a thermometer. Benadryl (or a generic) is good for bee or ant stings, itchy rashes, and other allergic reactions. (Benadryl is also good if a bee stings your pet.) Tylenol reduces fever. Ibuprofen (Motrin & others) reduces inflammation. However, if you are in basically good health and have a good immune system, you should try to eliminate Acetaminophen and Ibuprofen products (unless there is a fever).

Keep a Medical Journal

Get a spiral notebook and keep a medical journal. Make a section for each member of the family. You might want to include your pets. You can do it on the computer, but a spiral notebook is easier to take to the doctor. Or buy a calendar to use only for recording medical notes.

Every time anyone goes to the doctor, write the date, symptoms, what the doctor said, and medicine prescribed. You should also record the date and ALL symptoms that occur. Particularly if you begin a new medication, record any different feelings or sensations you experience.

Perhaps your child is complaining of leg pains. It is probably "growing pains" (something the medical profession doesn't always recognize), but it could be the beginning of something that wouldn't be significant enough for the doctor to diagnose until months later. Or perhaps your child had a bicycle accident (wasn't wearing a helmet) and three weeks later is having headaches. If you recorded that fall, you know exactly what to tell the doctor. Or what about a mild fever that comes and goes – you know how those "viral things" are. Write down when your children lose a tooth, when they go to the dentist or eye doctor. *Write it all down.*

How many times has the doctor asked, "How long have you been having these symptoms?" Unless that is the ONLY thing you have to think about, chances are very good you are not going to remember accurately. Time goes by so quickly, "Well, doc, I think it's been a week or two, but maybe it was two months ago."

Keep your journal in a handy place – and USE IT. It could prove invaluable. With the odd illnesses that crop up these days, it is wise to have a place where ALL symptoms have been recorded. Your doctor will be very impressed. An additional benefit will be having everything at your fingertips if you need to fill out paperwork for medical procedures or for insurance. And if, by the grace of God, you never need it for anything big, it will be a wonderful family medical history for you to pass on to your children some day.

Over Medicating

You might have seen news stories about over medicating in our country. For example, some children have had so much Tylenol that their illnesses no longer respond to it. The medications keep getting stronger.

Amoxicillin used to be the drug of choice for children's ear infections and other illnesses, but many older children cannot use it now. Why? Because it was prescribed even when the child was not really ill. Parents didn't want to chance another trip to the doctor's office, so they left happily with a prescription that wasn't needed.

So many people go to the doctor for a prescription because they believe pills will make everything better. Even though a virus must run its course, many patients want pills. Be informed. Talk to the doctor and actually listen to what he or she has to say. Unless they are the type (and some are) who write a prescription for everything, they will be happy to talk about alternative treatments (or waiting) instead of having another patient who blindly believes that pills are the only answer.

Don't take medications unless it is absolutely necessary. Don't take other people's medications, and be very careful about diagnosing yourself.

They Are Only Human

Take the time to evaluate; talk to other folks. It is tough to find a doctor these days who actually has the time to *care*. Whether it is the insurance companies or the sheer volume of patients they see every day, many doctors don't seem to have enough time to spend with their patients.

My doctor prescribed Wellbutrin along with blood pressure meds. On a TV commercial, I saw a Wellbutrin commercial that said, "This new product does not raise your blood pressure." I was not taking the new product. When I asked, I could see the answer in the doctor's face before he spoke. He *knew* this combination was not compatible. I didn't bother to mention that it was plainly stated in my records, the very folder he held in his hand – or to ask if this was why my blood pressure remained high. I changed doctors.

Another time, my triglycerides hit 2500 (should be below 150). YOU can prevent a lot of things from happening. YOU are in charge of what you eat and what kind of exercise you get. And you must be aware of medications and side effects. *Diuretics can dramatically raise your triglycerides if you have a severe sulfur allergy. (Refer to the "Physicians Desk Reference.")*

When you go to the doctor, here are some questions you might want to ask. Make sure you write the questions down and take the paper (or your journal) and pen with you into the doctor's office.

1) Do my symptoms mean something specific?
2) Is this new medication widely used? (Just because it is a free sample does not mean it is the best choice).
3) Is there a generic? Is the generic just as good?
4) What are the side effects (physical or emotional) of the medication?
5) Is there a less expensive, comparable medication?
6) Is this medication compatible with the other meds I am I am taking? (also ask your pharmacist this question)
7) Can these prescriptions be taken at the same time?
8) Can these prescriptions be taken with vitamins? (Never take aspirin and Vitamin C at the same time.)
9) Why do I need this test?
10) Is there any risk involved with my treatment?
11) Is there another option other than medication?
12) Will this medication limit any activities, foods, or driving?

For more information, go to the library or buy a PDR (Physician's Desk Reference) or search online and *check for yourself* when drugs are prescribed. Doctors can make mistakes. Do not go on blind faith – check for yourself.

When you get a new medication, always ask your pharma-cist about it. Ask about side effects. Pharmacists do more than just fill prescriptions; they know medications, reactions, and vitamins. They can also tell you about interactions between vitamins and pre-scriptions. Use all resources available to you. Check out all prescriptions at **www.rxlist.com.**

A Multi-Billion Dollar Industry

Many people are so conditioned to take doctor-prescribed medications that they will never consider a different approach – or question the doctor's diagnosis. While prescriptions are sometimes necessary, chemicals are *not* normal to the body. A combination of chemicals might fix one problem but cause other problems. Listen to the television commercials that advertise medications, and pay attention to the side effects that can occur. Some of the side effects sound worse than the original problem! And just look at all of the class action suits that lawyers are promoting against drug companies. Notice how, through commercials and magazine ads, we are encouraged to request additional medications but are rarely encouraged to change our eating habits to healthier choices.

The prescription drug industry is huge and getting richer every day. The more medications you take, the more money they make. While medications have helped many people, we need to be informed consumers: aware of possible problems, of side effects, and know that vitamin deficiencies and poor diet can be responsible for many illnesses. Don't choose chemicals when vitamins, better eating habits, and exercise could be the answer. Alternative medicine supporters believe most health problems are caused by vitamin and mineral deficiencies and are curable through diet.

Alternative Medicine

Alternative medicine is a growing field. Of course, there are times when you must take prescription drugs. If you have strep throat, it could prove fatal to wait for vitamins and herbals to work. However, in treating high cholesterol (for example), you should visit your local vitamin store for vitamin/mineral solutions and develop better eating habits before loading your body with prescriptions/chemicals. Given the right ingredients (and exercise), the body can do a wonderful job curing itself in many circumstances.

Many natural products work just as well or better than traditional medicine, but you must be careful; there are also horror stories. Many illnesses have similar symptoms. You don't want to die while you're experimenting with herbal remedies when what you really needed was a chest x-ray or a battery of blood tests to identify the hidden problem. Pay attention to what your body is telling you and don't wait too long to seek other opinions.

More MD's are going into holistic medicine. That means a medically trained doctor is treating with natural products when possible; they have realized that traditional medicine generally treats the result rather than addressing what caused the problem. Sometimes what might seem a major problem could be as minor as a severe vitamin or mineral deficiency. For example, arthritis flare-ups can be a direct reflection of eating certain (wrong) foods.

Here are a few things you might learn from a holistic MD: vitamin D deficiency can cause fatigue; acidophilus can improve a compromised immune system; vitamin B is important for muscles and nerves; the right amino acids may do a better job than prescription anti-depressants; magnesium is important for the heart, and much more. Of course, you need to know the correct dosage – which can only be identified through blood work. Only a doctor can tell you exactly what you should be taking.

Whether you are using traditional or alternative medicine, remember that it is the *practice* of medicine. While much progress has been made, doctors do not know how each body might react to the prescribed treatment. Always be aware of what your body is telling you, always question new procedures, investigate all aspects of your illness, and call your doctor if you have side effects.

What Is Your pH?

Do you know the difference between alkaline and acidic foods? Do you know that people who are ill (cancer, for example) generally have acidic bodies? Not surprisingly, non-healthy foods are acidic: soft drinks, white flour products, chemicals, prescription drugs, tobacco, fast foods, etc. Alkaline foods are most vegetables, most fruits, almonds, certain spices, etc. Your diet should not be 100% alkaline foods; you are seeking a good balance to maintain a healthy body. If you are ill and your body is acidic, you should concentrate on alkaline foods to bring your body into balance.

For a complete list of alkaline and acidic foods, go to www. essence-of-life.com/moreinfo/foodcharts.htm OR search on the computer for "food chart alkaline acidic." This search will bring up a number of websites that will give you a chart. Also, get some pH test strips. Check with your local vitamin store or search online for pH hydrion papers.

Juicing is a healthy choice. See **www.hacres.com** for an eye-opener. The Hallelujah Diet isn't the easiest plan – lots of juicing plus eating raw fruits and veggies, but there are many health benefits. My dad didn't like most vegetables but decided he could eat raw sweet potatoes. The age spots disappeared from his hands.

Remember that one source rarely has all the answers. Regardless of the subject matter, it is best to review all available information and use the parts you need.

How Is Your Posture?

Most of us stay slumped over something: the kitchen sink, the washing machine, the computer, the steering wheel of our cars, and so on. As a nation, our posture is poor. Poor posture affects the growth of the spine, and many people are experiencing more problems with their necks and backs than ever before.

While our lifestyles encourage slouching, have you ever noticed how people with rounded shoulders just don't have a successful air about them? They look tired and beaten down – even when smiling. Rounded shoulders put pressure on your neck and make you stand in an awkward manner. Compare that look with the stance of politicians, public speakers or career military folks, people who are "schooled" to look good in public. They stand straight, head up, and look proud. Some call it the look of success.

If you tend to slouch, take a minute to stand up against a wall with your head, shoulders and heels touching the wall. That will give you a reference point as to where your shoulders should be. Straighten up and look in the mirror. Good posture can make you look like you have lost five pounds! In the car, adjust your seat to sit upright. At the computer, raise the monitor if your neck is not straight, and take frequent breaks. Pay attention to your posture. It is something that can come back to haunt you.

A Word about Aging

When you are 20, older people seem old beyond belief. At 40, you still feel young. After 50, there are mysterious aches and pains. We know that our best years are behind us. But the worst part is how young our minds still feel. We wonder how all of those years passed – and so very quickly. If you're young, show respect and kindness for older folks. Your 80-year-old grandmother still feels she should be about 30. Honestly, time will pass much faster than you can even imagine!

Toothbrushes & Bathrooms

We know toothbrushes should be sterilized on occasion, particularly if you or a family member has been ill. To wash, put toothbrushes in the dishwasher or use soap and hot water. If a family member is sick, keep that toothbrush away from other toothbrushes. After a bad illness, doctors suggest replacing the toothbrush.

It is best to keep toothbrushes protected from bathroom air where dirt and germs tend to be. Of course, the toothbrush cover also needs to be sterilized regularly. To be on the safe side, flush the toilet with the lid down, and always wash your hands after using the bathroom.

Along with regular cleaning, spray the bathroom for germs and at least daily if someone is sick. Spray the doorknobs, light switch, faucet knobs, and the toilet and handle. In public restrooms, always wash your hands and use a paper towel to open the door.

A Few Healthful Hints

- If you cannot get warm, concentrate on your feet. If your feet are toasty, it is easier to warm up the rest of your body.
- Chewable Vitamin C can eat the enamel off your teeth, so can soft drinks and juices.
- Flossing your teeth every day is important.
- For hiccups, try a bite of peanut butter.
- For paper cuts, use a little "super glue" directly on the cut.
- For blemishes (zits), do NOT use hot water then "pop" them. Instead, use ice. Ice calms the skins and can resolve the problem. Put an ice cube in a plastic baggie and hold it on the spot or use a cold pack. As with anything, don't overdo it. Keep the ice on the "zit" for about five minutes. Facial skin is tender!
- For sinus problems, try using Vitamin C (with rose hips) instead of over-the-counter medicine.
- Use regular cornstarch for heat rashes.
- If mosquito bites swell, itch incessantly and become sores, try using a poison ivy product.
- Ice (or a cold pack) helps bug bites (especially stinging insect or spider bites). For sprains or muscle pulls, use ice only for 20 minutes at a time. (On for 20, off for 20)
- If you have extreme pain in your toe from an ingrown toe-nail, open a vitamin E capsule and put several large drops

on your toe and cover with a Band-Aid. You should have relief quickly. The nail may need to be cut later, but the vitamin E will soften it, making it easier to cut.

- Using anti-bacterial soap constantly has been shown to kill too much beneficial bacteria. Regular soap and warm water is the best bacteria fighter.

- Drink hot green tea. It is a wonderful antioxidant and has many health benefits.

- Reduce a fever by removing socks (cover feet loosely with a blanket), then put cold cloths on wrists, forehead, and back of neck. Rubbing alcohol is colder than water and can be used on cloths for stubborn fevers.

- Need a cold pack you can shape? Pour rubbing alcohol (it will not freeze solid) into a heavy-duty zip lock bag and freeze it.

- Deep breathing activates your immune system. Each day, take time to inhale slowly, hold your breath, then exhale. Try to take three big breaths at least three times a day. This is also an excellent way to relax your mind and body.

A Word about Beauty – Facing the Facts

With all the talk about diet and exercise and staying healthy, we can't forget skin. Take care of your skin, particularly your face. Of course, heredity makes a difference. Some women look magnificent at 65 – younger than others do at 45. However, to help fight aging: drink green tea, take fish oil capsules, take vitamin C, get enough sleep, drink lots of water, exercise, and don't smoke. A thyroid dysfunction can cause dry skin and premature aging. Don't forget about your hands; always wear rubber gloves when washing dishes!

Moisturizing is important. If your cleanser leaves your face feeling tight, it is too drying. While there are many good products on the market, my dermatologist suggested Cetaphil™, a good and inexpensive cleanser; however, it does not do the best job removing heavy foundation makeup. The natural mineral products keep your face cleaner, if you can use them. Be sure to always use a good, clean moisturizer on your face. While it might be difficult to believe when you are 25, some day you will be 50 and your face will reflect the care you gave it. Spend the money for quality facial products.

Chapter Thirteen
Diet & Exercise Tips
Watch and pray that you do not fall into temptation. The spirit is
willing, but the body is weak. Matthew 26:41

I Don't Want to Weigh This Much

For many years, I have been tired. This coincided with the birth of our first child, 20+ years ago. Before she went to pre-school, I was sleep-deprived because I ran a newsletter business from home and frequently began work at 11:00 p.m. after husband and baby went to sleep. With the birth of our second child, I knew I would never have enough sleep again. The first was a night owl; the second was an early riser.

Take a combination of not enough sleep, frustration, and stress (because it is hard to deal with things when you are sleep deprived), plus eating more – just to have enough energy to make it through the day – and what happens? Suddenly you are growing out of all your clothes! You head for the discount stores and buy bigger clothes, believing this is just a temporary thing – *until you get it all together again* – and you buy bigger clothes, then bigger again. Then you look in the mirror one day and guess what? That huge person really is you. Your last baby was born three (or five or ten) years ago, and you still look about seven months pregnant. In fact, just last week, somebody actually asked you when your baby was due! Not only is this weight unhealthy, but it will likely cause future health problems.

Recent medical research shows that sleep deprivation and stress contribute to weight problems. If you are having trouble sleeping, do not use the computer right before going to bed. The light from the computer tells your body it is time to wake up!

An underactive thyroid (hypothyroidism) can cause problems. Sometimes it is not severe enough to show up in traditional medical tests. Untreated, this can lead to problems with high blood pressure, high cholesterol, and your immune system. Symptoms include fatigue, depression, forgetfulness, weight gain, insomnia, dry skin, hair loss, and also problems with menstrual periods, hot flashes, and mood swings. (*Source: Ellen Kamhi, PhD, RN, Stony Brook University's School of Medicine*) You should always consult your doctor before self-diagnosing, and the right blood tests are the only way to know exactly what you need. If you like to check symptoms online, www.WebMD.com is a good site.

As you consider changes you need to make, remember it takes about four weeks to make or break a habit. That means, whether you are trying to start something good or stop doing something bad, you must give yourself time to develop a new habit. *Love yourself* and be kind and patient with yourself as you start on your new walk.

Write It Down

When trying to lose weight (or identify a food allergy), keeping a food journal is helpful because it makes us accountable. Use a small, easy-to-carry, spiral notebook. Nothing fancy needed – just write down everything you eat and drink each day. Also, note if you did any exercise that day. This is helpful so you will realize exactly what you are eating, and it is useful to record any problems experienced after eating certain foods. Also, it can help your doctor determine your reaction to certain foods and possible allergies – such as wheat, dairy, and gluten.

Exercise Can Be Fun

Some years ago, I received a phone call out of the blue. "Do you want this horse?" my uncle asked. I was beside myself with joy.

There was a beautiful and affordable pasture boarding facility near my house. The downside of that sixty acre spread was all the walking involved. Depending on which pasture the herd was in, I sometimes had to walk half a mile to get my horse, another half mile back to the feeding area, and another mile to return her to the pasture and get back to my car. That was two miles a day. She needed a special feeding program twice a day, so I began walking four miles a day without realizing it.

After a couple of weeks, people began asking what I was doing to lose weight. My clothes were feeling less tight, but I didn't pay much attention because the scale didn't show a loss; however, I was losing inches! I lost three dress sizes without trying! The scale didn't show it because muscle weighs more than fat. With all the walking I was doing, I was gaining muscle and losing fat.

If you are trying to lose weight, you probably know you should walk. But I never knew how *much* I needed to walk. For best results, you should walk about four miles a day. This can be broken up into several shorter walks if you can't do it all at one time. But remember that some walking is better than no walking! Walking will also lower blood pressure.

Find What's Right for You

Why can't I make myself walk? Are you a goal-directed person? It was easy for me to walk to the horse because I had a purpose. She was not going to eat unless I took the food to her. And she was always so happy to see me that I could hardly wait to go again. However, it is difficult for me to take time to walk down the street – purely for health/weight benefits – when I have so many other things I would rather do.

What do you do? Your health may be at risk. FIND what works best for you. If you need a treadmill or other exercise equipment, search garage sales and classified ads for used equipment. Look on www.craigslist.org and freecycle.com. Find a place to put a machine (some fold up to save space) or find a friend or neighbor to walk with you. Find what works best for you and get moving.

Exercise At Home

Here are a few simple ways you can build muscle tone and burn calories around the house. *(Always consult your doctor before starting any exercise program.)*

- Take throw rugs outside and beat them against a sturdy tree, fence post, etc. Really put your strength into it. Switch arms. Do this at least once a week and you will feel your stamina starting to improve. It also does wonders for stress relief. Your stress level and blood pressure might decrease if you give those rugs a daily beating!

- If you have stairs, whether to the upper level or to the basement, *use them.* People actually pay to use a "stair master" at a gym. Go up and down those stairs until you get your heart rate pumping, then give yourself a cool down period where you are slowly walking through the house until your heart rate returns to normal. Do not get your heart rate up and then sit on the sofa.

- When you go through a door, stop, turn sideways, and raise one arm up to the top of the door frame. It doesn't matter if you can't reach it; just stretch the muscles in your arm and side. Repeat with the other arm. It only takes a few seconds to do this. Get more benefit by doing a few repetitions. Make it a habit, and you will soon notice trimmer sides.

- Before you get out of bed, try to spend a few minutes stretching. Once out of bed, gently bend over and try to touch your toes; twist at the waist, do some arm circles. Start your day with movement.

- Walking clubs in malls can be fun. You can walk early in the morning before the stores open. Walkers go at their own pace. If you are close to a mall, call the management office for information. You might need a mall pass to come in before stores open. Walking the mall is great exercise and don't forget those stairs for a true cardio workout!

- Especially if you have problems with high blood pressure, it is important to get your arms moving above your heart. If you can't jump, do "stationary" jumping jacks and wave your arms back and forth over your head. Punch the air, do arm circles – whatever it takes to increase your heart rate. The arm exercises can also be done from a sitting position. For any type of exercise, stretch a little before starting and have a "cool down" time after raising your heart rate. Cool down by simply moving your arms at chest level (rather than over your head) for a minute.

Cutting Calories Painlessly

If you need to lose weight, do *not* think about how many times you might have tried with no lasting success. Do not think about any unkind thing that has ever been said to you. There are many different weight loss plans. You simply have to find the one that works for you.

The United States is now known as the having the highest number of obese people in the entire world. The weight problem knows no boundaries. It can affect anyone – from the very rich and famous to the very poor. I actually find some comfort in knowing that *Oprah Winfrey* fights the same weight battle that I do.

Many of us have paid for help in losing weight. Unfortunately, many of us have regained that weight. If you need to lose weight, understand that you *must* change the way you eat.

The problem with most diets is that you are *temporarily* eating food combinations you would not ordinarily choose. Therefore, when you go back to eating your preferred foods, you regain the weight. For successful weight loss, you *must* eat fewer calories, eat healthier foods (usually lower in calories), and get exercise. If you want chips, don't take the bag to your favorite chair! Put a handful of chips in a bowl and no refills. Concentrate on eating slowly and savoring each bite.

Eat healthy, but do not deny yourself the things you love – just eat less. A small, coffee cup-size of ice cream is just as satisfying as a big bowl. Actually, it is *more* satisfying because you know you are not eating all those extra calories. Make a cup of hot tea. It is calming and takes your mind off of eating. There are many wonderful, flavored, decaffeinated herbal teas. Green tea (use honey instead of sugar) is a very healthy choice.

To lose weight, you must eat fewer calories and get some exercise. For eating healthier and help losing weight, consider the following – fairly painless – suggestions:

- Until noon, eat only fruit. You can still have coffee or tea (don't forget water) – just no cooked foods. Green or herbal tea is a healthy choice. It won't matter if you occasionally have an egg, toast, etc. Just don't eat a stack of pancakes drowning in syrup.

- Eat slowly and chew your food thoroughly. That is better for your digestion, and you will feel full more quickly. Stop eating when you are full. Even though that sounds obvious, many of us continue eating long after we reach the "full" mark.

- Drink a glass of water before your meal. When you want to eat something, drink a glass of water first. Sometimes your body actually wants water instead of food.

- Do not eat dinner after 6pm. Actually, 5pm is better if you can do it. You can have a snack later, but no heavy foods at night. If you eat dinner (reasonable portions and no bread or pasta) early and have a light, low calorie snack or no snack (think about that tea!), you should see a difference on your scale the next morning. Add a little exercise (a walk after dinner) for even greater results. Beware of salty foods that cause water weight gain.

- If you use margarine, use a zero trans fat – no hydrogenated oil, "heart smart" margarine.

- Cut back on sugar, including sugary drinks. If you must drink cola, beware of diet colas. *See page 118 for more information on colas and diet colas.* Juices have a lot of sugar too; watch your calories and drink more water.

- For snacks, try carrots, cucumber slices, etc. If you get tired of eating them plain, use a small amount of Ranch dressing. Read labels. Some dressings contain high fructose corn syrup and a lot of salt, including fat-free products. Oil & red wine vinegar is a good choice, and some people use lemon juice. Balsamic vinegars are also a good choice.

- At home, pretend you are at a restaurant and serve yourself a "restaurant-sized" portion. No seconds!

- Salads are healthy choices. Raw foods are important. Eat leaf lettuces (not Iceberg) and add other things for interest. Grate carrots and/or raw sweet potato into your salad. Finely chopped broccoli does not taste strong and gives a great crunch to your salad. If using salad dressings, watch the calorie content on the label. Some salad dressings have as many calories as a hamburger and fries.

- Stay away from "white food": bread, rice, sugar, potatoes, and pasta. Try barley. Eat red potatoes instead of brown, wheat bread instead of white, and brown rice. You will see a better weight loss by cutting down your carb intake. Try eliminating bread and pasta and limiting other carbs to ½ – 1 cup sizes.

- If you have retain water, you may need to watch your salt. Red sauces, processed foods, chips, crackers, fast foods, and other salty restaurant food can make you retain water; this generally affects your blood pressure.

- Eat more leafy green vegetables. They are naturally low in fat and low in calories (unless cooked in grease), high in fiber, and loaded with vitamins your body needs.

- Instead of ice cream, get a glass of *ice-cold* skim milk (or vanilla almond milk). Either keep a mug in the freezer, or fill your glass and freeze for 10-15 minutes until it gets a little "slushy." Add a few drops of vanilla flavoring and a teaspoon of chocolate syrup if you want. It is almost as good as a dish of ice cream – better when you think of how many calories you have saved.

- Get tested for food allergies. An allergy to wheat, gluten, dairy, or other foods could be the reason you are having trouble losing weight.

- You can eat sweets, even every day (unless you know you can't). Just make sure you keep the portion small. Buy the 100 calories ice cream bars and snack packs.

- For many people, achieving peace, harmony, adequate rest, and a sense of purpose in your life is the key to successful weight loss and an overall healthier body. Getting enough sleep is extremely important.

If you remain significantly overweight, chances are good you *will* have future health problems. Knee and hip replacements, diabetes, high blood pressure (which will cause heart trouble), and a host of other possibilities are waiting for you.

"Laugh and the world laughs with you...."
Laughing is *really* important. Have you laughed today? Giggles don't count – a *real* laugh, a *belly* laugh. Just like exercise, laughing releases endorphins – the body's energy. If you haven't had a good laugh in a while, find something that really tickles your funny bone and LAUGH – long and loud. You will feel better instantly.

Some of us have more trouble laughing than others. In fact, some of can't find a darned thing to laugh about. We are too busy worrying about our problems. Sometimes we go to the doctor and get anti-depressants.

Anti-depressants can change your life. Used correctly, they can "take the edge off" and allow you to function in a happier state. However, you must realize that *the pills will not solve your problems*. If you are taking anti-depressants, are you also trying to resolve the difficulties that brought you to this point?

It is no secret that stress, unhappiness, and consistent lack of sleep can make you sick. Finding the answer to your problem is the key to regaining your health. And find things to make you laugh. Go out and rent the funniest movie you ever saw and watch it as many times as you can before it's due back!

He laughed his way to health

One of the greatest health stories of all time is about a man named Norman Cousins (1915-1990), known as "the man who laughed his way to health." In the mid-1960's, he developed Ankylosing Spondylitis, a fast-growing, fatal, degenerative disease that causes a breakdown of collagen (tissue that fastens the body's cells together). When he was almost completely paralyzed and given only a few months to live, Mr. Cousins decided to stop traditional medicine in favor of natural medicine. He also had a doctor friend who was willing to help him with his experiment.

With large doses of Vitamin C (in an IV drip) and large doses of laughter, he beat the illness. He watched hours of re-runs of *The Three Stooges* and other shows that he thought were hilarious. He watched anything that would generate real laughter from his body – and he beat the "fatal" illness.

Years later, he had a massive heart attack. Again, he laughed his way back to health. For inspirational reading, look for his two books: *Anatomy of an Illness* and *The Healing Heart*.

Chapter Fourteen
Cleaning Up & Maintaining
In all thy ways acknowledge him, and he shall direct thy paths.
Proverbs 3:6

CLOTHES & MORE
For years, television commercials have told us we need a pantry full of special cleaners. There's one for spots, one for spills, one for carpet, one for tile, and on it goes. If we bought every product advertised, we would spend hundreds of dollars on cleansers alone. Actually, you only need a few products to do just about *everything*. Here are some suggestions:

If clothes are really dirty, soak them. Put detergent in and run the washer for about five minutes, then turn off the machine and let the clothes sit overnight. Don't do this with colors that will run (bleed). Rather than buying fancy "enzyme" cleaners, try a half cup of liquid dishwasher soap in your load of dirty jeans. *Never use DISH soap in your washing machine, only dishwasher soap.* For stubborn spots, apply liquid dishwasher soap directly to the spot. Use an old toothbrush to work it into the stain. Let it sit for an hour or so, then wash.

Always check to see if the stain has come out BEFORE you put the item in the dryer. If you can't tell, hang the item to air dry so you can check the soiled area. Re-treat the stain if necessary.

Washing in cold water? What if the cold water wash is nothing more than a ploy to make you buy *more* products to clean your clothes? I finally decided it was cheaper to wash the dirtier clothes in warm water and stop buying additives. (If a clothing label says to wash in cold water, do so – or the clothing may shrink.)

Don't overload your washer. It is so tempting to stuff in that extra pair or two of jeans, but a packed washer cannot properly clean clothes. Even with a dryer sheet, your laundry won't come out smelling fresh if it is overcrowded. Another good freshener is to add a cup of baking soda OR white vinegar.

Sometimes a second rinse is needed. If a load of towels sours after sitting for a few hours (especially in warmer weather), you need either a second rinse or to use less soap. A second rinse cycle should remove most of the soap residue that makes the towels (or other heavy clothing) sour. Of course, clothes may sour if left in the washer overnight during warm weather.

Stubborn Stains

For particularly stubborn stains – especially grease stains, use liquid dishwasher soap. *Note: Dishwasher soap is not advertised as a stain remover. Use at your own risk. If it fades or damages the clothing, the responsibility is yours.*

When using dishwasher soap, rub it into the spot with an old toothbrush. For bad stains, let it set for a while; for minor stains, you can wash it right away. Liquid dishwasher soap is also effective for cleaning carpet stains, but be careful – you can lighten that area more than the rest of your carpet. After you have used it to clean the carpet, be sure to take clean water and go over the spot once more – to stop the "cleaning action." Soak up water (blot) with a towel.

Dried blood is more difficult to remove. Dishwasher soap might help; combine with Clorox Bleach Pen on white or beige items, and repeat as needed. Hydrogen peroxide works well to remove fresh bloodstains.

Clorox™ is good for bleaching whites and freshening your washer. Clorox Clean-Up™ is made for countertop stains, white letter tires, and more – and it also works for laundry. For anything <u>white</u>, including the items that say, "Do not bleach," it is wonderful for ring around the collar and cuffs, stained t-shirts, sheets, etc. You can use it on colored clothes, but the item MUST BE WET and you must be willing to throw it away if you ruin it. That is the last resort, knowing that the item is not usable as is. If you over-bleach, the item goes right in the trash because it was ruined anyway. *(Even though I personally use it on clothes, Clorox Clean-Up is not sold as a laundry product. You take full responsibility when you use it for something other than it is intended.)*

Urine Smells

Baking soda or white vinegar will neutralize a urine smell. Use one cup of soda OR vinegar – not both. Look for good deals on large sizes of store brands. Laundry detergent and warm water will take care of most smells. Overnight soaking is *very* effective – just be sure you don't soak colors that might run. Also important with extra dirty or smelly clothes–do not overload the washer. With more room to move around, the clothes have a better chance of getting clean. If the items have only been wet on *once*, you can probably get them clean in a regular laundry load. If the items (like bedding) have been wet on several times – they need extra attention. For cat urine, pour vinegar ON the spot.

Windex

Even before the movie, "*My Big, Fat, Greek Wedding*" came out, one of my favorite products was Windex™. Not only does it clean mirrors, windows, countertops, appliances, etc. – did you know it kills ants on contact? It won't keep them from coming back, but they are dead with the first squirt. It is also a great fly killer. Mid-air isn't good, but if the fly is at a window (or bathroom mirror), one good squirt of Windex and the fly drops – making it easy to finish it off with a paper towel. The added benefit here is, if you squirt the fly on your window, you can wash your window at the same time! Windex now makes a product that kills 99% of germs. *Do not use Windex on wood furniture.*

Although there are other glass cleaning products, I prefer the Windex brand.

Favorite Hints (listed in alphabetical order in Index)

• **PAINTING** – Need to stop painting but don't want to do a full clean up? Put your roller and/or brush in the paint tray and slide tray into a large white garbage bag. Secure the end with a twist tie. It will keep for several days. For longer periods, put it in the refrigerator. If only using a brush, secure brush in large baggie. If you need to leave the brush for more than a day, use a heavy-duty baggie.

• **OLD DRYER** – Is your dryer getting old and taking too long to dry? Do you frequently have to dry the loads twice – even when it isn't overloaded? Take your vacuum (must have a hose) and a crevice tool and vacuum the lint trap. If you don't have a crevice tool, make one with an empty paper towel roll and flatten the end enough to get it into the lint trap. Vacuum the lint trap as well as you possibly can. Unhook the big hose that vents the dryer outside and vacuum inside of it. Make sure your outside vent is clean. Long, flexible lint brushes work well and are generally available at hardware stores. *Lint-jammed dryers are a major cause of fire.*

• **SQUEAKY SHOES** – Have you ever had a pair of leather shoes that squeaked? An old horseman's trick for squeaky saddles (leather rubbing against leather) is to sprinkle baby powder on the spot. This is amazingly effective for shoes and sometimes works for hardwood floor squeaks.

• **BALL POINT PEN** – Marks on clothes? Rubbing alcohol will remove it, but it does take a little effort!

140

- **VACUUM SMELL** – Each time you vacuum, take one square of toilet tissue (or a cotton ball), spray it with cologne, and vacuum it into your machine. Works well in new or used bag. This would probably work equally well for a bagless vacuum. It leaves the house smelling so nice! Also, baking soda is a natural odor eater. Especially for heavy pet traffic areas, sprinkle baking soda and let sit for about 15 minutes to help absorb odors.
- **ANTS IN FLOWER POTS** – Have ants taken over a flowerpot and you can't kill them? Put 3 drops of dish soap in a gallon container, then fill with warm (not hot) water. Pour entire gallon through foliage and dirt. Ants can live and swim in plain water, but soap kills them. Because it's only a small amount of soap, it will not harm your plant. A good squeeze of dish soap is also effective for ant hills. I make a quick dig with the shovel, squeeze soap, then pour about 8 oz water into it.
- **DRY SHAMPOO** – No time to shampoo? A small bit of cornstarch rubbed into the greasy parts will absorb excess oil. Too much will turn your hair white! Comb or brush as normal.
- **CONDITIONER** – Especially if you have fine hair, when using conditioner, never apply it to the top of your head. Your hair becomes greasier, faster, at the part. Instead, try applying your conditioner about three inches from the top of your head. Especially if your hair is long, conditioning is needed more on the ends.
- **GUM IN HAIR OR ON FABRIC?** – Coat with peanut butter (NOT the crunchy kind). Also, WD-40 is effective at breaking down the properties in gum. If gum is on a tightly woven fabric, peanut butter might work – or try "freezing" the gum with an ice cube (put the ice in a baggie), then scrape off the residue with a blunt knife. Remove a grease stain with dishwasher gel product.
- **ROSES/WOODY STEMS** – When you cut roses (or any other woody stemmed plant), cut stems at an angle under running water. Hold your finger over the cut until you *quickly* place the stem in water. As soon as air reaches the cut, it starts sealing itself. Put a "flower fresh" packet in the vase – or pour a half can of Sprite in the water. Trim stems every few days to keep them fresh longer.
  For Christmas trees, trim tree then put in water as quickly as possible. Use Sprite or flower fresh packets as above.
- **PERSONAL PHONE BOOK** – Use a notebook/binder to hold all your telephone numbers. Each year when your children get their classroom directory, put it in the binder. Put your Sunday School class list in there, your subdivision list, your Christmas list.

Dividers (like for a school notebook) make things easy to find. If you have lots of personal numbers, get A-Z dividers so each letter has its own page. I do my lists on the computer for easy updating. Some blank notebook paper in the front of the book is always handy.

Write all your cell phone numbers on a separate sheet of paper. If your phone is lost or damaged, you won't lose your numbers! Keep a copy of that list in your binder and also in your car in case of emergency.

• **COBWEBS** – Frustrated with cobwebs around your ceiling? Get a "ceiling brush," a floppy rounded brush on a telescoping rod (you can lengthen & shorten the rod). The brush isn't stiff enough to damage anything; it is easy to clean, and it makes quick work of ceiling cobwebs. Or use the old-fashioned method: securely wrap and pin a thin cotton cloth (or old white t-shirt) around the floor end of a broom and use that for your cobwebs. Wash the cloth so it will be ready for your next use.

• **BATHROOM CLEANING** – Keep cleaning supplies in each bathroom. It is much easier to do a quick cleaning if you don't have to go gather supplies. Also, if a guest happens by unexpectedly, you can always excuse yourself for a few minutes to run to the bathroom and do a quick clean-up!

• **JEWELRY CLEANER** – for gold and precious stones: in a small glass, put 2 drops of dish detergent plus equal amounts of vinegar and water – enough to cover your jewelry, then stir. Soak rings, necklaces, or earrings for about 30 minutes. Use an old, soft toothbrush to gently scrub any stone settings, then rinse under running water. Your jewelry will sparkle! For a quick clean, spray ring with Windex and scrub gently with a wet toothbrush. If your ring is too tight and hard to remove, spray your finger with Windex. *Use the vinegar/water mix on jewelry that is at least 10K gold. Wash pearls only in soap and water. Personally, I think ammonia does a better job than vinegar, but vinegar works well and is something more people keep in the pantry.*

• **GASKETS ON REFRIGERATORS & FREEZERS** – Use dish detergent and water to clean your gaskets (the rubber part around the door that makes the door stay closed). If the refrigerator or freezer door doesn't seem to be sealing, smear Vaseline™ or other petroleum jelly over the entire gasket and close the door. Let it set for a few minutes, then open the door and wipe off *most* of the Vaseline. It cost us a $55 service call to learn that trick.

If you have used the Vaseline treatment several times and the door is not sealing, use Windex or soap & water to clean all Vaseline residue from the gasket. Dry thoroughly with paper towels, then coat with Vaseline as described above.

Preventive maintenance: wipe your gaskets with a wet cloth or sponge often (to keep gasket pliable) *before* you need the Vaseline treatment.

• **KITCHEN SPONGES** – Always "wash" your sponge in hot soapy water <u>before</u> using it to wipe counters or wash dishes. Sponges can also be washed in the washing machine (do not put in dryer) and in the dishwasher. Another way to sterilize your kitchen sponge: <u>wet it</u> and "cook" in the microwave for 45 seconds. It will be very hot when you take it out – and germ free. I microwave my sponge every day before using it.

• **CEILING FANS** – Most homes have at least one. A friend's baby had terrible allergy problems. The doctor asked, "Do you have a ceiling fan in the baby's room?" They did. "Don't run the fan at night," said the doctor. "Unless you want to dust the top of the fan blades every day, you are keeping the dust from *ever* settling in the room, and the baby stays in a dust cloud." He advised them to turn the fan *off* at night. The positive results were immediate.

Cleaning Fans: If the fan blades are thick with dust, use wet paper towels to clean off the mess. Once the blades are clean, you can use a "fan blade cleaning brush" once a week or so to keep them clean (or wipe with a wet paper towel). The fan brush is a brush with a hole in the middle of it that is the perfect size for a fan blade. Some have a "dust catcher" on them.

• **COMPRESSED AIR** – This is a must for blowing dust out of your computer or sewing machine. It is also handy for getting dust out of hard-to-reach areas, ornate picture frames, vents on your electronics, etc. (A vacuum hose with a brush can be used on those hard-to-reach items). Compressed air is great for a quick dusting if company calls to say they'll be there in 5 minutes!

• **CLOTHES SORTING** – Do you have children close to the same size or a problem with giving the wrong clothes to your children? Use colored fabric markers and make a small dot on the inside tag or neck band. Be sure it doesn't go through thin fabric. For white socks or underwear, make a dot on the sock toe or inside the waistband. Buy a different color marker for each child, and sorting clean clothes will be much easier – for you or for them!

- **CLOTHES SHRINKING** – If clothes shrink in the dryer, re-wet the item, then stretch it with your hands. For too-short pants or shirts/sleeves, pull to stretch the fabric then hang to dry. This won't work with all clothes, but it works for a lot of them.
- **MESH BAGS** – Buy large mesh laundry bags from the dollar store and tell your children to put dirty socks and underwear in the bag. Wash bag in the washer and put in dryer in your normal load, then return to your child to sort. I bought two bags for each child, one for socks and one for underwear. If the bag doesn't have a "handle," pin or sew a loop of ribbon on the end if they want to hang it over a doorknob.
- **SOCK SORTING** – Buy bags of one color socks for husbands and children. The socks are identical, so easier to sort (the mesh bag might still be the best solution for children). Use large safety pins to pin dress socks/specialty socks together and you will eliminate any problem with "orphan socks."
- **WATER HEATERS** – Water heaters have residue in the bottom of the container. To extend the life of the water heater, it should have a small amount drained out of the bottom at least once a year. Because this residue circulates through the water, never drink or cook with hot water from your faucet.
- **CAST IRON PANS** – If you have cast iron pans with baked-on food, put an inch of water in the pan and heat to boiling. Use a stainless steel brush (kitchen tool) to scour the pan. Dry, then place in warm oven. When thoroughly dry and cool, put small amount of cooking oil in pan and coat interior lightly using a paper towel. If food sits in a cast iron pan and rusts it, use an SOS pad to scrub out rust, then wash in hot, soapy water, put in warm oven to dry, and coat with oil.
- **HANDY MEASURING TAPE** – At the store and need to measure something? A dollar bill is approximately 6 inches long and makes an excellent substitute measuring tape.
- **FURNACE FILTERS** – Change them monthly if you are using heat or air conditioning.
- **WD-40** – Tired of losing the little straw that comes on some spray cans? Secure it to the side of a can with a rubber band. WD-40 is great for loosening most stickers.
- **KEEP MICE OUT** – If you know where they are coming in, stuff a pad of steel wool (any grade) into the hole or around where the pipe comes into the house. Mice will not chew through it.

• **GARDEN TIPS** – Some plants (bushes and trees) prefer acidic soil while others (annuals & vegetables) prefer alkaline soil. To check your soil, buy a soil testing kit.

Discourage weeds with landscape fabric or layers of newspaper (lay papers on ground then wet them to keep in place). Cover with pine straw or mulch. Remember that dirt will blow on top of the pine straw and it will break down over time. As weed seeds blow in, they will again take root but will be easier to remove. Keep a good base of mulch for easy weeding in the future.

• **GREAT YARD TOOL** – Go to a feed/equine supply store and buy a *pick* – the new pitchfork. The *pick* has a long handle and plastic tines. It is great for picking up pinecones, pine straw, leaves, etc. – anything you need to move into or from a pile. Also great as a rake, then flip it over and fill the wheelbarrow without using your hands or another tool.

WHAT IS IN YOUR TOOLBOX?

Useful toolbox items include: claw hammer, Phillips head screwdriver (for the star-shaped screw heads), flat head screwdriver (for screw heads with a straight line), measuring tape, and a pair of needle nose pliers (great for jewelry repairs and other small things). You can buy a combination screwdriver with interchangeable pieces that contain both types of screwdriver heads.

Other handy items might include a pair of large pliers, narrow screwdrivers (great for eyeglass repair, replacing watch batteries, etc.), duct tape, and black electrical tape. A container of one inch nails and picture-hanging hardware is handy, also a small level for hanging pictures, a tube of wallpaper paste if you have wallpaper (for repairing loose seams), and a rubber mallet – great to have when you need it! Superglue is handy; keep it well sealed. Spackle is useful for repairing nail holes or sheetrock repairs. Keep spackle well sealed and also in a zip lock bag because it dries out quickly.

PET TIPS
About Fleas

The absolute, best flea control is to vacuum every day. The benefit of a bagless vacuum is that you can dump the canister each time you vacuum as opposed to leaving the bag in the vacuum. Depending on how long it takes to fill the bag, fleas can hatch from eggs and make their way back into your carpet. If you have a bag vacuum and are having a major problem with fleas, buy some flea powder or Sevin Dust and vacuum that into your bag first. Any fleas or eggs you vacuum up will be killed.

A cat flea comb is very effective on cats and on shorthaired dogs. Crush the fleas or drop in soapy water. Fleas can't breathe soap.

Wet Doggie Tip

Hate it when it's raining and your dog becomes a wet, stinky mess? Use Baby Wipes for between-bath smells. Especially if you are expecting company and don't have time to freshen up the family dog, grab a baby wipe or two and rub all over the fur. It dries quickly and works great. Some people say to use dryer sheets, but those contain chemicals that could inflame your dog's skin or cause a reaction when he licks his fur.

The Cat Box

Cat litter is so expensive, yet such a necessity. If you have several inside cats, the price of litter really cuts into your budget. Sick of the cat box smell and tired of cleaning the box, I decided to try pine shavings. In horse barns, I've noticed the barn cats were very happy using horse shavings for their bathroom needs. I took a cardboard box (similar size to the cat box) and put shavings in it. That box sat next to the box with regular cat litter for four days. Then I replaced the cat litter with shavings, and they began using the shavings.

Benefits of using shavings:
(1) No more cat box odor, just a faint hint of pine. If there's a fresh uncovered pile, I scoop it out and dispose of it. The shavings are cheap enough to dump the whole box often.
(2) No more walking through all the cat litter tracked out on the floor. A small dustpan and brush quickly pick up shavings chips.
(3) No more dealing with heavy cat boxes. The shavings weigh only slightly more when wet than they do when dry. It is easy to just dump the box and refill it.
(5) A 40 lb. bag of shavings from a feed store should cost $5 to $6. Depending on how much you use, one bag should last several months – or get free shavings from a woodshop.

Pet Boo-Boos/Ammonia

If your cat or dog urinates in the house, NEVER use ammonia for clean up. If you have ever been in a house where animal spills were not properly cleaned – or in a barn prior to stall cleaning – or the old monkey houses at the zoo – you smelled ammonia. If you use ammonia to "clean," your pet will usually return to that same spot the next time it needs to relieve itself. For cleaning urine, put a few drops of dishwashing liquid in about 1-2 cups of warm water. Add a half cup of white vinegar. Wash the spot and blot (remove excess liquid) with a towel.

Pet Care

• Your pet should always have plenty of clean, fresh water. Don't forget to wash the bowl often. A slimy residue will build up.

• Baking soda can help remove pet odors from carpet. Sprinkle heavily, let it sit for 15 minutes or so, then vacuum.

• When changing brands of pet food, ALWAYS mix some of the new brand with some of the old food. If you change brands without the mixing process, it can cause stomach upset for your pet and more work for you to clean up the mess.

• Spending money on quality pet food might save you money on vet bills. Cheaper pet foods have "fillers" and less nutritious food. If you buy quality food for your animals, they will eat less food and have smaller and less smelly poop. Go to www.rotts-n-notts.com and look on the left side of the page for "Rate Your Dog's Food." Click on it for an eye-opening article.

• Flax seed – I began giving it to my horses to help them shed more quickly. I'm not sure if it helped them shed, but my old gelding (now 29) no longer shows signs of arthritis. If you have an arthritic dog, you might want to try adding flax seed (or ground flax meal) or fish oil capsules to his diet.

• Flax seed and fish oil are also good for the heart. An Exacto Knife is handy to open fish oil capsules and as a pill splitter. Puncture end of capsule, then squeeze oil onto pet food.

• My ten-year-old cat had vestibular syndrome. After the vet meds, she stopped making progress until I began giving her a daily (opened) fish oil capsule in her wet food. Her head will always be tilted, but she improved dramatically after the fish oil capsules were added to her diet.

• Tape jingling dog tags together with scotch (clear) tape.

• Ask your vet before you give your dog rawhide bones. Some rawhide products do not dissolve easily. If your dog tends to devour rawhide chunks rather than chewing on it like a pacifier, the chunks may cause a life-threatening intestinal blockage.

• If you have an outside dog, take your dog on long walks or to the dog park, make sure he/she is on heartworm medication. Although inside dogs can get heartworms, it is less likely because they spend little time outdoors. Heartworm treatments are very expensive and very hard on the animal. Don't take the chance!

• If your pet won't use the lovely new bed you bought, it could be the polyester cover. Try covering the bed with a cotton sheet, towel, or piece of fabric.

• Monthly flea applications are expensive for multiple pets. If you use Advantage, buy it in bulk. A 4oz tube (for dogs 55–100 lbs.) will treat two 50 lb. dogs or several cats. The formula is the same for dogs and cats, just a lesser amount for cats. There are many online companies with great prices. Some good websites for pets and horses are www.petsuppliesdelivered.com and www.jeffersequine.com.

Get a syringe (no needle) and use the correct dose. Look online (google "dosage for advantage") or check the package at your petstore for the correct dosage. Empty tube(s) into a small glass jar with a tight lid. Shake before using. Draw amount needed into syringe and apply to pet.

• Giving pills – *For cats*, some pills can be cut into small pieces and successfully hidden in a favorite food. Or buy a "pill popper" from a pet store or vet; it should cost around $6 and works basically like a syringe.

To use: one person holds the cat by the scruff of the neck (the way mama cats pick up kittens). Insert pill popper to back of the throat (so they can't spit it out) and push plunger.

For dogs, you can use the pill popper; however, most dogs will eat just about anything covered in a bit of peanut butter or cream cheese!

Chapter Fifteen
Organize Your House
Help, I Feel Overwhelmed!
In all thy ways acknowledge him, and he shall direct thy paths.
Proverbs 3:6

Is your house a mess all the time? Or are you the opposite: cleaning until you are exhausted, can't leave the house until everything is perfect – so you rarely leave?

Having a spotless house is impossible for me. It would be nice, but there are too many other things I actually enjoy doing. There will be plenty of time to have a spotless house once the children are grown.

But what if it is too messy? What if the clutter has reached overwhelming proportions? What if you are so depressed by all of the mess that you can't make any progress? Truly, it is hard to think clearly in the midst of loads of clutter!

Housecleaning Made Easier

Maybe your kitchen is full of dirty dishes. If you break it down, it takes about three minutes (or less) to unload the dishwasher. Fill the sink with hot, soapy water and load it with dishes that need to soak. Work your way around the kitchen. Once you get one counter cleaned, the kitchen will look so much better. Regardless of how messy your kitchen is, it can probably be cleaned in less than thirty minutes. If you sweep or vacuum the floor and shake out rugs, that will also make a big difference.

To clean your house, take one room at a time. If you go through and empty trash from every room in the house, you will know the trash is emptied – but it won't show as an improvement. If you spend fifteen minutes of dedicated time cleaning one room, you will be able to tell a difference. Before going to bed at night, take a few minutes to straighten the family room.

When you take something to a different room, make sure you don't get distracted while there. Put all of your effort into one room for a short time. The rest of your house might still be a mess, but you can go into that one clean room and relax. For some folks, a good schedule is to clean one room each day. You must find what works best for you. Don't forget that children of every age benefit from a few chores!

The Packrat

We all know people who never want to get rid of anything. They even keep things that are broken. I will always struggle with throwing things away, and it used to be a real problem. With so much junk, I couldn't find the things I needed, and our basement was a disaster area.

My rationale for keeping everything was that I always seemed to need it once I had thrown it away. Also, I'm forever using a bit of this or that to create something new or embellish a school project for the children. Whenever we need to make a project, we go to the basement to see what we can find.

But at that time, things were out of control in the basement. Underneath the biggest pile was a pool table my husband hadn't seen for about five years. I prayed for motivation to clean the basement.

My prayer was answered when we couldn't decide what to do for our daughter's fifteenth birthday. She wanted a boy/girl party, and we couldn't afford to rent a place. We had to use *The Basement*.

I approached the huge mess with a sense of urgency. Prior trips to the basement had left me feeling overwhelmed. This time, I had a deadline. I threw myself into it full force, worked in one area at a time so I could see progress, and was able to organize, throw things away, and repack.

The Fire

Part of my motivation came from a friend's fire. She had a small house and a very large pony barn. The barn was actually an old 1930s schoolhouse redone with precious pony-sized stalls, artistically decorated child-themed areas, an auditorium where we held the annual Christmas pageant, and a separate wing for her husband's business.

Also in the barn was an oversized room where she housed her treasures. It held extras from the house, a lifetime of family photos, her sewing machine, loads of fabric, all of the costumes and props for the Christmas pageant, and so on. It was her guest room, her storage area, her basement, her attic, her "everything" room.

One night, the barn caught fire and burned to the ground. Thankfully, only one pony was unable to get out (she had second degree burns from trying to move the pony). I was crushed for her that she had lost all her treasures – all her mementoes, all the things she had saved for so many years – her "life." But she was much more upset about the pony, and it started me to thinking.

Her loss caused me to look long and hard at all of my junk, much of which hadn't been touched for years. There were some projects I would never complete, others I would never start. And so much paper – newspapers, magazines, and more. What would happen if I lost all of it? How devastated would I really be?

My choice was not to have a yard sale. Instead, I made five main piles. One pile was to keep (later organized, boxed and labeled); one was "undecided." One pile was trash; one pile was to offer to friends or put on www.freecycle.com, and the rest (of still-usable items) went to a charitable organization. Once I started, I was surprised at how quickly it went. It took the better part of a week, but my hard work paid off; the party was great AND we had a clean basement!

Get Rid of It

The moral to this story is it's okay to keep some things. But be sure you're keeping the *right* things. Do you have stacks of magazines that you know, deep in your heart, you will never read? Do you have old recipes you will never use? Are there stacks of expired coupons? Sewing patterns with pieces missing? Puzzles with pieces missing? Things that have needed repair – for years on end?

Are you storing the bed you slept in as a child, knowing it is really a piece of junk that nobody else would want? Don't let your life be cluttered with things that are *only* things. Do you really *need* all of those things? Are piles of clutter and broken things making you happy? Is it improving your life or the life of your family? Are you keeping things that could be cheaply replaced?

Some organizational experts say to toss unused items after three months and certainly to throw out anything you haven't used within one year. But that isn't a good plan for everyone. Get rid of it if you haven't used it for over a year and can't see a real need for it – or if it is causing problems in your home space.

We Need a Puppet Tonight

Many years ago, I bought a rabbit jacket with a detachable hood. I never used the fur hood but couldn't bear to part with it and, for 25+ years, it had a home in the top of my closet.

When my daughter was in fourth grade, she needed a beaver animal puppet for a school project. She wanted to go to a local pet store where they sold animal puppets for $20. "*Everybody* is buying one," she said (like I was going to fall for that one). But I remembered the fur hood. We put a rubber band a few inches from one end, forming a neck. Then we cut out a tail from cardboard, painted it black and hot-glued it to the back end. She had a wonderful FREE beaver puppet, and the teacher was very impressed with her creation.

The hood was an example of something I just didn't want to throw away. It wasn't hurting anything by staying in the top of my closet. If something had happened to it, I would not have been crushed. But if you have stacks everywhere, it IS affecting you. It can add to depression. Besides, if you can't ever find what you are looking for, why have it?

Remember the fire. What would happen if you lost all of those things? What would be most precious to you? What are the things that *really matter* in your life?

How to Let Go

If your things are around you in stacks, get some containers. I prefer the clear plastic bins, but boxes are fine too. For boxes, go to a liquor store (Friday afternoon is a good time), and they will have LOTS of small boxes. Put everything in boxes and label them (top of my closet, coat closet, my junk drawer, etc.). At your leisure, go through one box at a time. Perhaps you could make a deal with yourself to go through one box each night – or a few boxes each week. It is easy to get caught up in memories as you find old pictures and keepsakes.

Technology has changed the value of some things. I used to save newspapers for important headlines. Do you know what? Nobody cares about information you can easily find on the computer. My treasures were just another pile of papers that attracted bugs and would help fuel a fire. I threw them out.

For a while, I was keeping everything because of the collector craze. Metal lunchboxes were selling for obscene amounts of money – and who could forget the Beanie Baby fiasco? Regardless of what the "collectable" is, *someone* will make money on it at some point – but maybe not in your lifetime. It's kind of like playing the stock market. You have to sell at the right time.

What about the *Antiques Roadshow*? We watch and drool – but do you have any idea how many people they see? How few people actually make it on the show? Yes, a few folks have been lucky – but don't let that keep you from de-cluttering your house. If you really think you have things that might be of value, check with a reputable antique store. Or get a book from the library. You might get your answer on e-Bay. A few folks actually have treasure, but most of us just have junk.

Speaking of junk, you don't have to throw away everything at one time. As I made my piles, I re-thought my decisions as I went back through the "undecided" stack. Seeing everything again, I decided there were some things I really wanted to keep and other things I honestly did not need.

At a local estate sale, there were a ridiculous amount of collectibles. This woman had collected *everything*. I have never in my life seen such a quantity of things – and the heirs had already taken what they wanted. Most houses would not even have enough space to display all these things! I commented to one of the shoppers, "This is exactly why I have quit collecting things. I don't want it to look like this when I pass on."

On a personal note, I think my material detachment is also due to a renewed, stronger belief in God. When I leave this world, it isn't going to matter whether I had Lenox china or a no-name brand. Great-grandmother's china may end up in a yard sale some day, and that's okay. It should be owned by someone who will enjoy it. Having possessions, just for the sake of having them, isn't really what is important. If you are thinking that your collection – of whatever – is going to be your retirement fund, check out e-Bay. Your collection might be worth a lot less than you think.

Giving and Receiving Gifts

Does part of your junk consist of gifts you have received but don't like? Things you would have never bought for yourself, but you hate to throw them away?

Make a "wish list" and tape it inside a cabinet door. Then, when a holiday or birthday is approaching, your husband, kids, friends or family will know exactly what you would like to have! Keep a list for other family members, and encourage friends to keep a list, too.

Re-gifting is only appropriate if the item is new and is something you honestly believe the receiver would appreciate.

Unless you are sure of the person's tastes, do not give something that requires display. Candy, flowers, or gift cards always work. And don't forget the ever-popular Gift Basket (*pages 39-41*).

Chapter Sixteen
Keep Your Vehicle Running
*Faith is being sure of what we hope for and certain of
what we do not see. Hebrews 11:1*

Pay attention to your vehicle. It will generally "tell" you if something is wrong. If it's slow to start, your battery may be going bad. Have it checked *before* you get stranded. If it's making a strange noise, ask your mechanic for advice. If the *Check Engine* light is on, don't wait until you have a major (expensive) problem; go ahead and get it checked.

Especially if you drive an older vehicle, buy a pair of good jumper cables. A good set will last a long time and should not have any hazardous connections in the future. Instructions on using jumper cables are found in this chapter. If your tires are old, keep a can of "Fix-A-Flat" (or similar product) in your trunk, too.

Go Through the Checklist
If you drive an older vehicle, go through the checklist twice a month. Make a note on your calendar. On the first day and the fifteenth day of the month, check out your vehicle. For newer ones, every three months should be fine.

The Basic Maintenance Checklist lists things you should check regularly. If you don't know where everything is located, have someone show you. If you still have your owner's manual, most answers will be in there.

If you don't have anyone to ask, there are nice guys at the auto parts places. Buy a quart of oil (ask them what kind to buy), then ask one of them to show you how to check and add oil. Even if you don't need oil, they can still show you how to do it. While you have the hood open, ask him where the other things are. If you need new wiper blades, he will be happy to put them on.

BASIC MAINTENANCE CHECKLIST
Your car should be parked on level ground before you check fluids, and it is best if the engine is cold.
• **Check your oil**. If your car runs out of oil, it will destroy your engine. Your oil and oil filter should be changed every 3,000 miles if you sit in heavy traffic and around 4-5,000 miles for lighter

driving. An old mechanic once said, "Oil is the life blood of your engine. Clean oil is like having a healthy heart."

The oil stick is usually the most prominent "stick." Have a paper towel or rag handy. Pull out the stick and wipe it with the paper towel. Put the stick back in all the way, then pull it out and see where the oil comes on the stick. The stick has an "add" mark and a "full" mark. If the oil is only slightly below the full mark, you do not need to add oil. Or you might need to add *some* oil but not the entire bottle. Just pour some in, wait a bit, then do your "stick test" again.

DO NOT overfill the oil. A funnel can help you pour oil without spilling. If you spill, oil can make your engine smoke while it is burning off the residue; however, it doesn't cause any damage. Wipe off spills with a paper towel or rag.

• **Check the coolant** (antifreeze). In summer, this greenish liquid keeps your engine from overheating. In winter, the right mixture of antifreeze will keep your radiator from freezing. *This is important.* Check antifreeze *with the vehicle running,* but check it while the engine is still "cold" – before you have driven anywhere. Start the engine, then unscrew the radiator cap and look inside. The water level should be just below the neck of the tank (where the cap screws on). If the water level is down, carefully add some water but do not fill it all the way up to the top.

NOTE: Never remove the radiator cap when the engine is overheating. If the gauge in your car shows it is overheating, pull off to the side of the road and stop the vehicle. If the radiator is making noises (like a tea kettle), do not open the hood until the engine has cooled. *Antifreeze is poisonous to humans and pets.*

• **Check the power steering fluid** (look for the "add" line). Use a rag or paper towel to wipe off the residue and re-insert the stick just like you did with the oil.

• **Check the brake fluid** (look for the "add" line). Same directions as above.

• **Check battery terminals for corrosion.** Battery terminals can become corroded. The terminals are those short posts that stick out of the top of the battery; the battery cables are connected to them. You might see white, powdery residue on the terminals. This is called corrosion (the same powder you see if you leave batteries in a flashlight too long). The corrosion will eventually keep your battery from getting power (current). To clean the terminals, put a few teaspoons of baking soda on each terminal and pour a small amount of water on it. It will sizzle. Take an old toothbrush and scrub it a little. Use more water to wash the baking soda and corrosion off the battery. Be sure to wash your hands with soap when you finish.

If you are away from home and your vehicle fails to start, with a corroded battery as the culprit, you can pour cola (dark cola) on the terminals. It should eat away enough corrosion to let you get the engine started again, although you may need jumper cables because you probably wore down the battery trying to start it. (Yes, you may ask what the cola is doing to your body.)

• **Check the alignment/have tires rotated**. If your tires are wearing unevenly, your vehicle is probably in need of alignment. If your vehicle runs rough on some roads, your tires might need to be rotated. Tires should be rotated about every 7,500 miles. If your car is out of alignment, tires will wear out more quickly. If your vehicle seems to pull to the right (or left), it could need an alignment. Your mechanic can properly advise you.

• **Check the tire pressure**. Buy a good quality tire gauge to keep in your vehicle. If you don't know how to use it, ask someone to show you. The correct air pressure is printed on your tire (small print). It will say something like "40 psi." If tires are under- or over-inflated, they will wear unevenly and you will need new tires more quickly. Improper air pressure is unsafe, especially in rainy or other bad road conditions. Also, it will decrease your gas mileage.

• **Check the lights and blinkers**, front and back. The easiest way to check is to have someone walk to the front and rear of the vehicle as you test all your lights, but you can do it by yourself.

At night, pull up to any wall, fence, front of a store, etc. Check headlights, then high beams. You can see the reflection. Check your left blinker, then your right blinker. Now you are ready to do the back lights.

The back of the vehicle has more lights. They are very important because they give information to the person driving behind you. At night, back up to a wall, fence, etc. While looking in your rearview and/or side mirror, step on the brake to make sure both brake lights are working. Check both blinkers. Turn on your headlights to make sure the "night" taillights are working. Finally, put the car in reverse (with your foot firmly on the brake) to make sure your "back up" lights are working.

MORE TIPS

- If you are running low on gas, turn off your air conditioner and slow down. The air conditioner (A/C) can make your engine work harder and use more gas. Studies show that on short trips, running your A/C uses more gas. For expressway driving, the A/C uses less gas than having windows down. If your car is overheating, turn off your A/C.

- When starting your car, turn to ON and wait 15 seconds before starting. Let your car idle a minute after starting before you turn on the heat, A/C, or defroster.

- Before changing gears, come to a complete stop – or you will be buying a new transmission too soon! Always use your emergency brake when you turn off your car. Even a slight slope puts pressure on the transmission; it will last much longer if you use the emergency brake.

- Windshield wipers should be replaced when they smear the windshield. If the weather is very hot and dry, you can make wipers last longer by wiping the rubber part often with ArmorAll. ArmorAll wipes are very handy or use the spray bottle and a paper towel.

- Use less gas by reducing your speed. Accelerate slowly from a stop, and try to slow down gradually if you are coming to a red traffic light or stop sign.

- Keep your gasoline above 1/4 tank. If you had an emergency or were caught in a bad traffic jam, you might run out of gas.

- If your car quits and you leave the hazard lights (flashers) on, your battery will still be working. If you are gone for any length of time, you will probably need jumper cables and assistance to start the car again.

- Many vehicles now have some kind of magnetic decal. We proudly show the American flag and causes we support along with soccer balls, baseballs, tennis balls, cheerleader megaphones, and more. Move the decals to different places on your car because the sun will bleach out your paint. Move the decal(s) at least once a month.

- Vehicles have a gauge or "trouble light" that shows if the battery is charging. If your trouble light is on or if the gauge is reading to the left (negative) side of the mark, your engine is draining power from your battery. Turn off the A/C and radio. If daytime, turn off headlights. Get to a safe place or auto parts store because your engine can quit. Do not turn your vehicle off until you are where you want to be, because it probably won't start again with that battery.

  Jumper cables can offer a temporary solution; however, your battery probably needs to be replaced and you might need a new alternator. With a charge, a dead battery should make it to a nearby repair shop.

Using Jumper Cables

Check for battery corrosion (refer to pages 155-156).

Pull the running car (car #1) up to the car that needs the jump (car #2). Car #1 will be running the entire time. Open both hoods. Attach the positive (+) cable (red wire or red handle) to (+) battery terminal in car #1 and the other end to (+) terminal in car #2. Attach the negative (–) cable (black wire or black handle) to battery terminal in car #1. Attach the other black-handled wire to a piece of metal if possible or to the negative terminal in car #2. Make SURE you have attached it positive to positive and negative to negative (or metal). The negative cable is the "ground" wire.

You may get sparks when you make the last connection. In some cars, it might be hard to find metal, but sometimes the battery "cage" (that holds the battery in place) will have a metal bracket.

If your battery is dead because the lights were left on, it should only take a few minutes before car #2 starts. Remember that car #1 runs the entire time. If car #2 doesn't start, let it continue receiving the battery charge for 10-20 minutes. If it doesn't start after 3 or 4 tries, do NOT try to start it over and over because you will flood the engine. At this point, you will need to call a tow truck.

Driving Safely – Basic Tips

- Always use your blinker so other drivers know your plans.

- Slower drivers should always stay to the right. The left lane is for passing. You are not in charge of monitoring the speed of other drivers. Just get out of the way.

- Children belong in the back seat in their seat belts or car seats. If your vehicle has air bags, the manufacturers warn that children aged 12 and under can be *killed* when the front seat air bag deploys at 80 mph.

- Always wear your seat belt. Most accidents happen within a few miles of your home.

- Pedestrians (people walking) always have the right of way.

- Cell Phones: Research says drivers on cell phones respond the same as a drunk driver. If you must use your cell phone while driving, stay in the right lane so you don't impede the flow of traffic – or pull off the road to finish your call.

- Do not use Cruise Control when it is raining; your vehicle is more likely to hydroplane.

- Use traffic lights. If you need to make a left turn out of a store or gas station and have a choice of crossing busy lanes of traffic OR using a traffic light to easily make the left turn, please use the light. Do not take the chance of endangering yourself or others.

- When it is raining, turn your lights on. At dusk or dawn, turn your lights on. Driving with your lights on is <u>not</u> so you can see well. It is so *other drivers* can see <u>you</u>! Gray, red, and dark colored vehicles without lights on are even more difficult to see at dusk, sunrise, or in bad weather.

- Lights on during the day: Studies show that the subconscious mind is more aware of car lights in the daytime than of vehicles without lights on. To minimize your chance of an accident, drive with your lights on during the day.

- YIELD means let the other traffic go ahead of you. A YIELD sign leading onto a road with two right lanes means you *wait* until the oncoming traffic is finished – even though there are two lanes. If there is a sign that says "Keep Moving," you don't have to stop.

- When coming to a stop, always stop far enough back to see the full wheels of the vehicle in front of you. That way, if the car behind happens to bump into you, it won't push you into the car in front – and the policeman called to the accident won't give you a ticket for following too close.

- Starting a car requires a lot of power from the battery. A car must run about 30 minutes for the battery to fully recharge. Short trips weaken and discharge your battery.

- When you get an oil change, always check your oil. On occasion, shops have forgotten to add oil. If you smell something burning, have your oil filter checked. Filters can go bad and cause oil to leak out.

- LEADING & FOLLOWING on multi-lane roads: When someone needs to follow you, this technique makes it much safer and less stressful. When the leader needs to change lanes, the lead car signals (puts on his blinker) and <u>waits</u> until the second car acknowledges (puts on his blinker) and then changes lanes. The second car leaves space for the lead car to safely move into position in front of the second car. If there are three cars, the first car signals (puts on his blinker), then the second car signals the third car (with his blinker), and the first two wait until the third car can safely change lanes– thereby clearing a space for the two cars in front to move over.

    The lead car must watch traffic lights and never leave the second (or third) car if possible. If the lead car gets separated, that car should pull off to the side of the road and watch for the other car(s) to catch up.

Chapter Seventeen
Bloom Where You're Planted

*Happiness comes to those who are fair to others and
are always just and good. Psalms 106:3*

Something to Think About...

- If you use the right words, your words are a blessing.
- Listen more than you talk. You never know what you might learn. Look at everyone as a potential learning source.
- The respect you give others will return to you ten-fold.
- If you have no respect for yourself, you will not be able to show true respect for others nor will you act in such a way that others will have respect for you.
- A nice person who doesn't show respect for *all* others isn't really a nice person.
- Don't promise something unless you *know* you will do it.
- Ask "What do you think about...?" instead of being so anxious to say "I think" or "I want."
- Controlling your reaction to stressful events is more important than avoiding them. Look for positive ways to respond.
- Take responsibility – don't look for someone to blame.
- Take one day at a time. Separate worries from concerns.
- Be kind. People may not remember exactly what you said or did, but they will always remember how you made them feel.
- Don't tell people how smart you are. If you're smart, folks will figure it out. Same goes for your kids and grandkids.
- Be able to let go. Bitterness only hurts you.
- Read the instructions BEFORE you begin the project.
- If you expect the worst, you will seldom be disappointed.
- Practice random acts of kindness.
- In matters of humanity, being kind is more important than being right.
- If you always do what you've always done, you'll always get what you've always gotten.
- Happy people may not have the best of everything, but they make the best of everything they have.
- Don't forget to thank God for your blessings each day.

Bloom Where You're Planted

You may have heard that saying, but what does it mean?

A simple answer is: *Be thankful for what you have and do the best you can with it.* Stop complaining. Stop wishing things were different. Appreciate what you have. If you want things to change, try doing the very best with what you currently have. The Lord seems to favor those who appreciate and take care of what they have. A great quote is: ***Happy people may not have the best of everything, but they make the best of everything they have.***

It is easy to sit and complain, especially when you see people who seem healthy and wealthy but who cheat and lie and live as they please. Hopefully, you believe in evil, in Satan, because he works hard every day. His job is to show you that *his* way is not only more lucrative than God's way but is a whole lot more fun. There are many healthy and wealthy Godly men and women. God gave us free will to choose Him (and eternity with Him) or to choose the other (sometimes easier) path. Remember the "you reap what you sow" verse. How we choose to live is going to come back to us at some point. We *will* be held accountable.

Count your blessings each day. Praise God for what you have, take care of what you have, and thank Him in advance for the blessings He has planned for you in the future.

Be not deceived; God is not mocked: for whatsoever a man soweth, that shall he also reap. Galations 6:7

Where Is Your Faith Level?

Do you find it hard to pray? Do you feel like God isn't listening? Do you worry that you do not have *enough* faith? If you are praying, you have enough faith! Jesus said any amount of faith, even as small as a mustard seed, was sufficient. *See Matthew 17:14-20.* Find a church that will lead you in a more faithful path.

If you are a long time Christian and feel that your faith/spirituality/prayer life have weakened over the years, it might help to find someone who is new in the faith, someone who still has that child-like faith, someone whose belief is strong, whose faith is active.

Some "old time" Christians have lost their spark. They carp and complain, criticize and condemn, rarely mention God, listen to and tell offensive jokes, curse, and drink to excess. In short, they are no longer trying to "live as Jesus did." You can *say* you are a Christian but if you are not *living* it, it doesn't count. "Walk the walk; talk the talk." We have all heard that phrase and, if the Holy Spirit is <u>not</u> living inside of you, you will have no desire to walk and talk as the Bible commands.

If your church is not preaching the Word of God, find one that does. If the church youth group your teenaged child attends is not actively promoting virginity, find one that does. If your young child cannot easily recite Bible stories or Sunday's lesson to you, find a church with more spiritual teachers.

The Word is out there. Your job is to find it.

"Oh My God"

Do you, as a practicing Christian, keep the Ten Commandments? You are probably good on the not murdering, not worshipping graven images, not committing adultery, etc., but what about not taking the Lord's name in vain?

People who profess to be strong Christians say, "Oh my God" and "Oh Lord" without giving it a second thought. It sounds particularly offensive to hear young children use that phrase. Is that the same as *honoring God?* By using His name in place of what could be a foul thing to say? We honor God by using His name in prayer and in praise. As you strive to strengthen your spiritual awareness, consider the words you are using.

Are You Ready For a Miracle?

What about illnesses? Do you believe you can be cured? Do you believe others can be cured? Do you believe God will deliver you from your problem? Do you believe you must ask for His will, guidance, and wisdom?

If you are sick, it is your *body* that is sick, not your spirit. Say, "Lord, my body has a problem but my spirit is strong and will heal my problem." It will only work if you actually believe it! If you have a more serious health issue, concentrate on getting better. Tell your body it is improving. Thank God in advance for your healing. Visualize the medicine/vitamins/healthy foods helping your blood cells grow stronger and attack the problem in your body. Make sure you are only putting healthy foods and drink into your body, and dwell on positive, encouraging thoughts to maximize your healing.

Some people are so attached to their problems that they talk about them all the time to everyone who will listen, giving that illness/problem power over them. They have claimed their problem as if it were a blessing: MY arthritis, MY heart problems, MY bad child, MY bad luck, and so on. If you want to get well, if you want things to improve, you must stop claiming your problems!

Do you *really* believe in miracles? People pray for miracles and when something good happens, many pick it apart trying to find a human answer. "Expect a Miracle" is seen on all types of Christian products, but do *you* expect a miracle? Or do you pray, doubting all the while that it will do any good – as you continue to worry? *According to your faith be it unto you. (Matthew 9:29)*

Too many times, we hold onto our problems. We want help, but we can't seem to relinquish our control. Let go. Let the Lord have it. Of course, you know you *cannot* take it back. You cannot say, "Lord, I don't know what to do. I give you this problem," and five minutes later when your friend calls, you are telling her about it – again. If you are asking your friends for help and advice every time you get the chance, that is *not* giving your problem to the Lord.

When we trust in the Lord, we get answers. Sometimes the answer is yes; sometimes the answer is no. Sometimes we don't hear anything – and we might think he has forgotten us. But those are the times when we must wait. We know the right answer is accompanied by an inner peace – the peace that passes understanding. If you force a wrong solution, you will likely end up with a bigger mess.

Most of us know Godly men and women who suffer from an assortment of illnesses and problems. Hardest of all is to see children suffer. Few things are as difficult as living a devout life while you suffer or watch a loved one suffer, and it is crushing to see someone pass when so much prayer has been offered. Though always beyond our comprehension, we know that good people do suffer and pass away. Our job is to keep their memory alive, to support good works they believed in, and to trust that the Lord made the right choice – as we pray "Thy will be done." We must trust that, even though it wasn't *our* choice, the person's work here was done and it was time for them to return home.

Remember there is power in the spoken word, so keep your words positive. While we don't always see the miracle we wanted, we might never know the positive impact that experience had on someone else's life. We must trust that things have happened for the best. *And we know that all things work together for good to them that love God, to them that are called according to his purpose. Romans 8:28*

Can't and Won't

Do you know the difference? Many people confuse these two words. *Can't* generally involves a definite answer. For example, *I can't go to work because I have the flu.* Or, *I can't write because I have a broken finger. I can't come to your party because my child's concert is that same night.* You get the idea.

Won't, however, is an entirely different word. People often say *can't* when they really mean *won't*. Examples would be: I can't stop smoking (won't). I can't stop drinking (won't). I can't control my children (won't). I can't lose weight because I can't find time to exercise. Sorry – won't and won't!

Do you see a pattern here? *Won't* involves *effort.* It takes *effort* to stop smoking or drinking. It takes *effort* to discipline your children. It takes *effort* to lose weight or stay on an exercise program. In fact, the sample sentences *should* read: *I just won't put forth the effort necessary to ____.* The responsibility belongs to you.

Sometimes, we need help. We might need patches to stop smoking. We might need AA to stop drinking. We might need professional counseling to save our marriage or to regain control of our children. We might need other programs to get us on track to lose weight or exercise regularly. It is good to seek help, to recognize that a change needs to be made, to know you don't have to do it alone. Regardless of what type professional help you are getting, ask God to help too.

When You Need Help

God has much more experience helping people resolve their problems than anyone else ever could. I don't know why anyone would try to do it without Him. If He is not an active presence in your life, find a church that will help you know Him – or pray this simple prayer all by yourself:

> *Heavenly Father, please come into my heart and*
> *forgive me of my sins. I believe you sent your son,*
> *Jesus, to save me. Please send the Holy Spirit to*
> *reside within me and fill me with your peace. Amen*

If you sincerely want His help in changing your life, it is going to take a little effort. Asking God into your life is only the first step. To truly make a difference, you must make God a real part of your life. Reading the Bible is important. Get an NIV Bible (easier to understand). If money is a problem, buy it at a thrift store. If you can get a study Bible (with explanations of passages), that is even better. Read the Bible each day. Make time for God each day, just as you want Him to make time for you.

Until I made time for God each day, my life was stagnant. Just praying was not enough. Once I began reading the Bible, I could see my life starting to improve. I chose to start with Matthew and read the New Testament first. If you want to use the computer, try www.Bible.com and follow their "read the Bible in a year" program.

Nothing is Perfect

Many people are turned off from religion – from churches and other groups – because people have disappointed them. "Those people" did not treat you right. They ignored you, didn't welcome you and left you out even when you volunteered your special skill. Worse, they appeared to sit in judgment over you. So you decided to leave them, to be alone.

Unfortunately, some Christians develop an arrogant, "better than," behavior. Do they really believe they are right to ignore and condemn others? Matthew 7:1 says, "Judge not" and cannot be misinterpreted. While there are always people looking to condemn or control others (not just in churches), there are many more great folks out there looking for new friends. Visit other churches.

If you often have difficulty in new situations, the problem could be yours. No situation will be perfect. Instead of waiting for others to reach out to you, try reaching out to them. Let them know you are friendly and happy to be there. Look for the best in everyone. Listen instead of talking. Don't begin by confiding your many problems (seen as wanting pity). Your new friends have problems too, but they are enjoying this opportunity to forget their troubles while they socialize and worship. Remember:

(1) These are regular people – just like you. They are in church to improve their spiritual life and to find friends who have interests similar to theirs.

(2) We should not turn away from God. If one church does not provide what you need, visit other churches until you find the place where you feel peace and acceptance.

(3) Yes, you *can* be spiritual without being in church; it just gets a little lonely sometimes. Look for a women's Bible class (or Circle) where you can learn more about the Bible and meet new friends.

Are Your Words A Blessing?

Do you find yourself thinking about what is wrong in your life instead of what is right? Do you complain (maybe constantly) about your problems? In complaining and holding onto negative thoughts, *you might be cursing your life.* As long as you continue to do this, your situation generally will not improve.

There is power in your thoughts and in your spoken words. Try to eliminate negative thoughts from your mind, and do not speak negative words. Speak words of encouragement – to yourself and to others. If your words are not a blessing, you are not using the right words!

Each day when you wake up, speak a blessing on your life. Bless your house, bless your family, bless your body, bless your friends, bless all things that have meaning in your life – especially the things that are giving you problems. Only by changing your outlook – your attitude – can you improve your life. By speaking encouraging words, you can push negative issues away.

"It's Me, It's Me, O Lord"

Do you know this old hymn? *It's me, it's me, O Lord, standing in the need of prayer…not my brother, not my sister, but it's me, O Lord, standing in the need of prayer.* While there seems to be a movement to discard the old hymns, there are many we should review often.

This particular hymn is a great reminder that we need to pray for God to change *us.* We need to realize that we might be the problem, not the other person. Instead of praying, "Lord, I hate my boss; make him go away," try praying, "Lord, please help me understand this person. Show me if I am wrong; show me how I might improve the situation." It is perfectly acceptable, however, to pray that the boss gets a better opportunity elsewhere!

Pray for God to change you to help you handle other situations: trouble with your marriage or children, parents, friends, etc. Sometimes it is necessary for you to change in order to change the other person.

Always pray for others: for their health, their safety, their well-being, but also pray that YOU are making the right choices, that you are not contributing to the problem.

Never ask God to change someone else without first asking Him to change you.

"Help Somebody Today"

Yes, it's another old hymn: *Look all around you, find someone in need, help somebody today, though it be little, a neighborly deed, help somebody today....*

The best way to stop thinking about *your* troubles is to help someone else. It is amazing how therapeutic this can be. Choose carefully. It doesn't count if you bring a meat dish to a vegetarian! You must help others in the way *they* need help – and in a way that is respectful of their situation.

The Bible tells us to do good works and keep them secret *(Matthew 6:1)*, but I will include this story as an example of a random act of kindness. When I have some extra money, I like to help folks buy groceries. I try to keep it as quiet as possible and do not wait around to be thanked.

One special experience was on a December 30 during a quick trip to the grocery store. I only needed a few items but kept meeting an elderly lady in the aisles. I felt drawn to her and finally said, "Okay, Lord, I think you want me to help this lady. Show me how." When I went to the checkout, only one register was open, and the frail little lady was in front of me. The cashier rang up her meager purchases: two cans of black-eyed peas, a frozen pack of collards, and a few other carefully chosen items. (Black-eyed peas and collards are traditional Southern food for New Year's Day.)

As the lady slowly counted out her food stamps, I took a deep breath (hoping I wasn't going to offend her) and said to the cashier, "I would like to pay for her groceries."

The lady was totally overwhelmed – and so was the cashier. "Nothing like this has ever happened to me," she said. Then she started to cry, so I started to cry. Her thank you's were embarrassing, so I wished her a happy new year, gave her a package of quick-sale chicken (she wasn't buying any meat), and went on my way. I imagined her getting home and calling her friends to say, "You'll never guess what happened to me today!" I know it made her day special, but it made my day great, too. It was a wonderful feeling to give that much joy for under $20.

Whether you are the giver or the receiver, there is nothing better than a random act of kindness.

A cheerful look brings joy to the heart, and good news gives health to the bones. Proverbs 15:30

Free Will

Free will is probably one of our biggest mysteries. It would have been so much easier if God had simply made us "good." But just as He gave Adam and Eve free will *and instructions,* He gave us the same. Our job is to *choose* to do the right thing. By reading the instructions (the Bible), we are prepared to go forward in life. When we choose to turn away from those instructions, we suffer consequences. For help interpreting the instructions, find a good, Bible-based church.

Seven Deadly Sins

Many years ago, Mahatma Gandhi listed the seven deadly sins. They are just as true today:

> Wealth without work
> Pleasure without conscience
> Knowledge without character
> Commerce without morality
> Science without humanity
> Politics without principle
> Worship without sacrifice

Change Your Attitude

A mom and her daughter went into a store to do some shopping. The mom was already in a bad mood and, not surprisingly, she had a problem with the cashier. When they were on their way back to the car, the mom said, "Did you see the look that cashier gave me?" The daughter replied, "She didn't give it to you, Mom. You had it when you went in."

We all have challenges from time to time, but that does not qualify as an excuse to put a scowl on our faces and pass along negativity to everyone in our paths. A humble spirit allows us to see others as more important than ourselves, and that humbleness will change our attitude if we let it. How can you be grumpy when you are trying to help someone else in need?

When you are having a bad day, look for opportunities to help others. Look for ways to serve instead of demanding that others cater to you. *Be kinder than necessary (J.M. Barrie),* and try to break free from aggravations that can ruin your day.

Most of us are much more concerned about ourselves than anything else. We worry about things we cannot change, all the while forgetting we can change what matters most – the one thing that controls everything else: our attitude.

Sitting in Judgment

Jesus said, *"Do not judge, or you too will be judged. For in the same way you judge others, you will be judged, and with the measure you use, it will be measured to you."* Matthew 7:1-2

Too often, we are guilty of judging others. Through gossip and casual comments, we proceed to pass judgment on the rest of the world. Some people seem to spend most of their time judging others.

The passage in Matthew goes on to say, *"Why do you look at the speck of sawdust in your brother's eye and pay no attention to the plank in your own eye?...You hypocrite, first take the plank out of your own eye, and then you will see clearly to remove the speck from your brother's eye."* Matthew 7:3-5

We cannot control the world. We cannot control other people. We cannot control what has gone before us nor what will come after us. If we can just keep *ourselves* (and our children) under control, that is a full time job. We are not responsible for the behavior of others, and we are not here to sit in judgment over them. The Bible tells us to respect our governing authorities, and those authorities are responsible for the judgment and punishment of people who are actually in need of being judged.

There will always be people we do not want as our best friends. Perhaps we are concerned they might be a negative influence on our children or our marriage, or maybe their personality just doesn't match well with ours. Whatever the case, we should still be considerate and respectful of others. That doesn't mean we must invite them for Sunday dinner.

Our responsibility is to lead by example, to make choices that are righteous, and to share the Bible and good works with others without sitting in judgment.

Managing Anger

If you start the day with a positive attitude, if you strive to be forgiving and helpful to others, if you remove from your thoughts any desire to "get even" with others – verbally or physically, you will be a much happier person.

So many problems began with the wrong words – or worse, with someone who *thought* they were wronged and then were too stubborn to let it go. *A fool gives full vent to his anger, but a wise man keeps himself under control. Proverbs 29:11*

Anger requires a lot of energy. You must be on guard constantly, watchful for any wrong you think might be directed at you. If you really think about it, what we fear most is what frequently comes to pass. Dwelling on negative situations seems to draw those problems *to* us – it certainly never improves the situation.

We can choose peace or we can choose anger. It is *always* our choice, and it is our responsibility to choose to handle every situation in a positive way.

Dear brothers, don't ever forget that it is best to listen much, speak little, and not become angry; for anger doesn't make us good, as God demands that we must be. James 1:19-20

Kindness is a Virtue

In my life, I have been blessed to know some genuinely kind people. They are the people who listen, try to understand, and help in whatever way they are able – without judging and without expecting anything in return.

Genuine kindness is shown through warmth, patience, gratitude, and doing for others. Those who routinely show kindness find they are frequently the recipients of kindness. When you are kind to someone, your "payback" probably will not come from that person. Instead, your good deed might be returned when a stranger stops to change your flat tire or when someone returns your lost purse with the money and cell phone still in it.

Beware of manipulators – those who pretend to be kind only because they are expecting a favor; their intention is to establish a debt that must be repaid. Manipulative kindness is when you feel forced to do something out of a sense of guilt, against your will, or because it will serve a particular interest.

Difficult people can present a special challenge. During stressful times, it might be helpful to remember they "are often unhappy people who...awkwardly and desperately try to be accepted" *(The Power of Kindness by Piero Ferrucci)*. Some are frustrated by poor decisions they have made and are constantly trying to prove themselves; some merely enjoy making jokes at the expense of others, and some just seem mad at the world. To respond with kindness can be a challenge.

In most situations, being kind is more important than being right. Think about the end result. What will make *you* feel better? If someone is being exceptionally difficult, it is better to walk away than to engage in a war of words. If someone trashes you in front of others, the audience will view the aggressor as the problem, not you. By being kind (sometimes through silence), many sticky situations can be defused, and the angry person has a chance to think about whether or not his actions were the right ones.

When corrections must be made, think how you would want someone to talk with you if the situation were reversed. You would want them to treat you with kindness and allow you to keep your dignity. We should always be as kind as possible. While people often don't remember the details, they will always remember how we made them feel.

A church choir director was much loved by everyone. Life experiences had made her an expert in many areas, but that wasn't what drew people to her. The people knew her as a great listener who never sat in judgment and could offer sound advice or insight for almost any situation. I marveled at how she didn't correct others just to show superiority. Corrections were made only if it truly mattered and then, always with kindness. She was a master of the *being kind is more important than being right* concept.

Most of us would do well to heed that same philosophy. More than anything else today, people need kindness from others. This is also a good time to mention respect again, because respect and kindness go hand in hand. It is said that kindness is the one thing you can't give away – because it keeps coming back to you. The same goes for respect. As you give respect to others, you are more likely to receive respect. By treating others with kindness and respect, you are living a life of example. You are helping others learn, and you are living a life that is pleasing to God.

All a man's ways seem innocent to him, but motives are weighed by the Lord. Proverbs 16:2

Favorite Scriptures

A heart at peace gives life to the body, but envy rots the bones.
~Proverbs 12:5

The Lord is near to all who call on Him, to all who call on
Him in truth. *~Psalm 145:18*

If you forgive men when they sin against you, your heavenly Father
will also forgive you. But if you do not forgive men their sins, your
Father will not forgive your sins. *~Matthew 6:14-15*

Trust in the Lord with all your heart and lean not on your own
understanding; in all your ways acknowledge Him, and He will
make your paths straight. *~Proverbs 3:5-6*

A cheerful look brings joy to the heart, and good news gives health
to the bones. *~Proverbs 15:30*

Jesus said, "Whoever can be trusted with very little can also be
trusted with much, and whoever is dishonest with very little will also
be dishonest with much." *~Luke 16:10*

Delight yourself in the Lord and He will give you the desires
of your heart. *~Psalm 37-4*

Jesus said to them, "Watch out! Be on your guard against all kinds
of greed; a man's life does not consist in the abundance of his
possessions. *~Luke 12:15*

The wisdom that comes from heaven is first of all pure; then
peace-loving, considerate, submissive, full of mercy and good fruit,
impartial and sincere. *~James 3:17*

Finally, brothers, whatever is true, whatever is noble, whatever is
right, whatever is pure, whatever is lovely, whatever is admirable –
if anything is excellent or praiseworthy – think about such things.
~Philippians 4:8

Commit to the Lord whatever you do, and your plans will succeed.
~Proverbs 16:3

173

APPENDIX

CHILDREN'S DANCE CLASS

Girls from the age 3-4 class and the 4-5 year old class did well. The parents of the "almost 3's" said their kids really, really wanted to do it; however, the children cried and complained about noise from the tap shoes. Age 3 is old enough if the child is a mature 3 year old and can pay attention.

Because a child's attention span is so short, we did ballet and tap. The class was an hour, and the shoe change was a good break. A little treat (candy) at the end of class was appreciated by the children. Gymnastic mats seemed a good idea (for basic tumbling), but I quickly realized that you actually need to know something about tumbling or someone's child could get hurt. I thought every kid knew how to do a somersault until one child performed an awkward maneuver that looked like she was going to snap her neck. I sold the mats – no more tumbling.

To prepare routines, I used the basic ballet positions and found some beginner ballet tapes at the library. Creating routines was my biggest challenge, but I kept them simple and repetitive, with a few drill team steps thrown in. The girls really enjoyed the "roll off." A most helpful teaching technique was to have the children clap their hands to the rhythm of the songs. This set the beat for them.

Use music the children know (one tap number was to *Sesame Street*'s "Rubber Ducky"), along with some simple classical pieces. Also, use some Christian children's music ("If I Were a Butterfly" worked well for floating around the stage) and some praise songs. Each song should only be 2 to 3 minutes long.

The recitals were so much fun. We had beautiful, reasonably priced costumes, ALL of the girls danced, and they did a great job. I had two classes. One class did their ballet number, then changed into tap shoes while the second class did their ballet dance. Backstage moms and big sisters kept everything moving right on schedule while I danced out front. Even though the children knew the routine, they were young. A three-panel, hinged screen provided the perfect answer. I was mostly hidden from the audience, but the girls could see me dance.

Check the Internet for wholesale dance costumes. You should find precious outfits at reasonable prices. Or use a leotard and matching net tutu. Pass the savings on to the parents or supplement your income.

Our stage was decorated with a donated balloon arch (not necessary but the girls loved it), and each family was asked to bring a dozen cookies or other sweets to share. We had plenty of food, and I provided the punch and paper goods. Each class performed to three songs: a praise song that was mostly hand/arm motions, a classical ballet piece, and an upbeat tap number. While the recital itself was short, the visiting time afterward made it a memorable event.

I ran my dance studio alone for two years. Our practice space had linoleum-over-concrete floors with no mirrors (mirrors would have been nice), and no ballet bar (we used the backs of chairs).

In 1996, I charged $25 a month and gave $5 per student (per month) back to the church. We did not discuss rent, so the $5 was rent/good will, whatever. With 15 students ($20 each), I made $300 per month for having two, one-hour classes a week. I also put in a number of hours at home selecting music and working out routines. If you can't find tracks of the music you want to use, you must find someone to record the music – you might have to pay them, or perhaps one of the moms plays piano and could do it for you.

To set your price, check the going rate for dance classes in your area. Consider "overhead" (paying for space + utilities) that big studios must include in their prices. If you work from a church (or other non-dance space), you should be able to get a good deal on rent – maybe free rent.

The downside of the dance classes (there is always a downside) was some of the parents. Most were absolutely wonderful, but there were always one or two who were anywhere from 10 to 30 minutes late. You might need to have a penalty payment for those who are habitually late.

Caution: Plan to have a helper – not because you need one, but because you should protect yourself legally. We live in times when people are too quick to accuse someone, even based on what a small child might say. It is beyond shocking to be accused of something when you didn't even know there was a problem!

I loved the children and it was easy to be patient because you knew they were only there for an hour! Just remember you *must* be patient, and you *must* keep things moving and keep it interesting.

MAKE MORE MONEY AT YOUR YARD SALE
SIGNS
- Keep your signs simple with large bold print. People cannot read small print as they are driving down the road at 35 to 55 mph.
- Use the same color of paper for all your signs and a thick, black marker. Even if they cannot read the sign, they will follow the color.
- Make one sign and put it about 20 feet away to see if you can read it before you make the other signs. Make sure you have plenty of signs, even large arrows work well.
- Keep your sign from bending in the wind. Duct tape a paint stick or clothes hanger on the back for support.
- More buyers are attracted to a "Multi-Family" sale. Serious garage-sale folks may not stop at a sale with only a few items showing – or mostly clothing. Go in with a friend or neighbor to have more merchandise to show.

PREPARING

- Put larger items (like furniture) out front to attract customers.
- Try to put smaller items on tables. If you don't have enough tables, use your coffee table (put a "Not for Sale" sign on it). Use heavy-duty boxes, turned upside down. Make shelves by running boards between two ladders or put a board between kitchen chairs.
- Clothing can be laid on a blanket – it's better if it is all the same price. Tape a sign to the front of the blanket.
- Hanging clothes – Garage door tracks make a great clothes hanger. Or tie a strong rope across your garage, carport, or between trees. Tie it high, because the weight of the clothes will pull it low. Use a ladder for center support. If you have a lot of clothes to hang, make several shorter "clotheslines." A long metal pole suspended between two ladders makes a great clothes rack.
- Seeing lots of clothing is a turnoff for some shoppers. Try grouping the clothing – women's clothes in one area, children's in another. Or boys clothes on one side, girls on the other.
- Group items together that are alike. Put all kitchen things together, all glassware together, all tools together, etc.
- Little toys are a great seller. Many parents bring children to sales and are happy to spend 25¢ or 50¢ to make the little ones happy. Consider keeping a cooler of frozen popsicles that your children can sell for 25¢ each. Some folks sell cold soft drinks or bottled water for 50¢ each.
- How to price? If you try to sell your items at almost new prices, you will be keeping much of your merchandise. People go to garage sales because they are looking for bargains. If you want to get rid of as much as possible, mark it cheap. Some sellers mark everything half price the last two hours of the sale, just so they will (hopefully) have little left over. Put up signs telling when items will be half price, and people might return later.
- Before you begin, decide how firm you want to be on your prices. This is especially important if you are having a sale with someone else. If you leave, they need to know how much negotiating room there is – or be able to stay in touch by cell phone.
- For pricier items, write the prices and a brief description of the item on a piece of paper. Although it probably doesn't happen often, there are people who will switch stickers. If you know your friend had a $15 sticker on her crystal bowl but here's a customer who says it's $1, you can refer to your "Price List." To the shopper, you say, "Oh, I am so sorry. Someone must have switched the stickers. I'm sure you can see that an expensive bowl like this would cost more than $1."
- Be very nice to everyone. You want them to come to your next sale too!

OFFICE HELP – INTRO LETTER

Prepare – or have a friend help you prepare – your personal letterhead. Your letter should be nicely centered/balanced on the page. Margins: top 1", bottom 1", sides 1½". Use Times New Roman font.

CENTER YOUR NAME, ADDRESS, PHONE NUMBER, ETC.:

Your Name (make this a little larger than the other type)

Your Full Address (123 Okay Road • Town, XX 12345)

Your Telephone Number

Your email address (if you have one)

(Use this space to balance your letter – equal white space between here and the bottom of the page.)

Date

(4 returns between date and salutation (Greetings) or company name. If you include company name & address, add 2 more spaces between that and "Dear...")

ABC Company
1111 Any Highway
City, AA 12345

Greetings:

Thank you for this opportunity to introduce myself. I am seeking a part-time position with a company in this area.

If you have any particular qualifications, list them. For example: I have some previous office experience and can answer telephones, file, send faxes, make photocopies, do light computer work, and schedule appointments. I am available to work *(list days, times, etc.).*

If you do not have any qualifications, someone might be willing to teach you. Write something like: I am a fast learner, a hard worker, and am very dependable. I would appreciate the opportunity to learn about office work.

Thank you for your consideration. I look forward to hearing from you.

Sincerely yours,

(4 returns – so there is room to sign your name)

Your Name (typed)

Always sign your name – do not photocopy your signature because it looks unprofessional. It is best to sign photocopies with blue ink to show it is an original signature.

PHOTOGRAPHY

Digital vs. SLR: I do not use a digital camera for photo shoots. I enjoy using an SLR and have good results from it. While I would love to have a high end digital, I cannot afford it. For now, I use my Nikon SLR and a digital for backup photos. Digitals are like magic and, granted, it is nice to see your results instantly.

If you are using an SLR (single lens reflex), you *must* have a good camera: Nikon, Canon, and Minolta are good names. Check with camera repair shops for refurbished models at reduced prices – and hopefully, a warranty. SLR's are harder to find, but you might get a good deal on eBay. Be sure to check the seller's feedback score!

An SLR camera lets you change lenses and add special filters. You need a zoom lens that goes from 30-80 (or higher). If you DO plan to get a digital, there are brands where the lenses are interchangeable with your SLR. Check with a reputable camera shop.

Special filters are available at camera shops, and those filters can add so much to your work. I like the "soft focus" filter, which softens the face just a bit. Grandma will particularly like the pictures you take of her with your soft focus filter! Another one is the "star" filter which is beautiful for Christmas tree shots and anything else that has sparkle. It will turn a sparkling evening gown into a gorgeous light display. An amber-colored filter adds warmth to your photo.

This is important – have your pictures developed at a reliable processing place. This can mean your local pharmacy. There are fancy, more expensive places; however, their work is not necessarily better, the staff only slightly more knowledgeable (sometimes), and the prices are certainly higher. Unless I need prints, I have a CD made. Always use "One Hour" – do not take the chance of sending out your pictures; they could get lost.

Printing from a CD may eliminate problems mentioned below:

Printing from SLR negatives: If you are sure you centered the shot but it's off center when you get your prints, check the negative. Sometimes the printing machines get "off center" and print differently than the negative shows. The store should reprint it at no additional charge.

Lint: Do you see white "hairs" or things that look like scratches on your photo? That is especially difficult to remove in the winter because those squiggles are lint or dust that is attracted to the photo paper by static electricity. A careless employee won't take time to make sure ALL the lint is off – because most customers don't care, don't notice, or don't know it can be fixed. Photos should be reprinted at no cost to you.

Red Eye: Have you ever taken photos where people (or animals) came out with glowing red eyes? The best way to eliminate this is to make sure you have PLENTY of light. Using a flash in a dark room will almost guarantee red eye – particularly for blue-eyed people. Even lots of light can leave shadows. Your camera's built-in flash will adjust to the lighting in the room and provide only enough flash to remove shadows from your subject's face – which is *exactly* what you want! Red eye can generally be corrected on the "picture machine" when you print pictures from a CD.

Photography Jobs – The Portfolio

When you feel confident to go out on your own, you need a portfolio to show examples of your work. Offer to photograph for free: babies, children, pets, horses, etc. Give the parents/owners some of the great photos to show your appreciation for the free advertising it will give you. If someone you know is getting married, go and take pictures. Stick close to the wedding photographer and learn as much as you can about how he/she groups people, where their hands are, etc. If you have friends in the wedding party, they shouldn't mind you taking pictures – as long as you don't interfere with the paid photographer. (Always ask for permission.)

Get a nice photo album to hold your "sample" pictures. Have some enlarged to 5 x 7 or to 8 x 10. Use clear plastic document protector sheets to hold 8 x 10s.

ASA 100 or 200 is best. Never use higher than 400.

The Working Photographer
Weddings

Weddings can be a little scary because if you mess up using an SLR, the happy couple won't have any pictures. Of course, digital cameras remove most of that fear.

If you are not familiar with the room, check out the lighting – preferably at the time the wedding or reception will be held – and shoot a 12 exposure roll of film to check the light and background. The camera sees things differently from the human eye.

For the event, make sure your main camera is in good working condition. Get out your manual and *make sure* every setting is where it is supposed to be. That might sound ridiculous, but I made a huge mess photographing a horse show (lost money on that one). I thought my camera was broken until I started checking settings. I never figured out what really happened.

It is best to have a backup camera. You need extra batteries for your flash, extra batteries for both cameras and, with an SLR, five more rolls of film than you think you might use. I generally shoot five to seven rolls at a wedding & reception, but I have shot as many as eleven. For most people, pictures from a digital camera would be totally acceptable. You could use your SLR for special shots.

Market*:* What do you want to shoot? Large weddings are tough for one person to photograph. You really need a qualified assistant and good equipment.

Smaller weddings are good, especially second (or third) weddings where they want lovely memories but not tons of photos. Also, in the smaller, more intimate atmosphere, the participants are not as panic-stricken.

Advertise: Give flyers or business cards to all churches in the area you are willing to travel. Leave business cards at bridal shops, bridal consignment shops, tux rental shops, and florists. And tell your friends.

Fees: There are two ways to approach this: (1) have all pictures put on CD and charge accordingly for your time and the processing (whether using film or digital) (2) have all pictures printed (stamp each one with "draft" or something so they cannot be scanned), and the couple orders reprints from you. Perhaps you would offer a CD option. I use plan #1. Visit photographers' websites for comparison pricing.

At The Wedding
WORDS OF WARNING:
(1)   If using an SLR, watch your film counter. If you're on #20 (of a 24 exp. role) and the service is starting, change rolls NOW. Better to have a roll a few photos short than to be in the middle of the service and miss an important shot because you're busy (noisily) rewinding and replacing film. Or – use your second camera.

(2)   Watch your background. The candles might make a lovely backdrop, but we have a wonderful wedding shot where the flames coming out of my husband's head make him look like the devil incarnate. Paying attention to background makes the difference between a professional and an amateur.

(3)   Have the bride write out a list of pictures she definitely wants. This will mostly be the people she wants to have in pictures. You will take:

Pre-wedding: bride getting ready, posed "candid" shots with her mom and bridesmaids, the reception area *before* guests come in so you can get clean shots of the tables and the cake(s). Some brides don't want all the pictures done before the ceremony, so take whatever you can. You might be able to do the groomsmen shots, the groom with his dad, best man, with the preacher, etc. Use your imagination. Take a picture of the bride's dad with his pockets pulled out ("spent all the money").

Ceremony: the bride standing in the foyer and in the doorway with her dad (take several of those). I generally take full length, mid-length, and close-up; however, new technology has made it possible to easily zoom in and crop. If you're using a digital camera, take pictures of everything. Get a shot of each bridesmaid and groomsmen as they come in. Take several shots of the flower girl and/or ring bearer. Take a shot from the back of the church (or hall) with the entire wedding party in it before the service really gets started. You can use a flash when parents light the unity candle, but you should not use a flash on any other photos taken during the service – unless that has been cleared with the bride/groom and preacher. You can recreate some of the more important photos after the ceremony: candle lighting, ring exchange, first kiss (they like to practice that one).

After the ceremony: When finished with the wedding party, ask if there are any other families who would like their photos taken.

At the reception, take all the usuals: cake cutting, first bite (discourage them shoving it in each other's faces because the bride's makeup is then ruined – *discuss this prior to the wedding*), garter removal & toss, bouquet toss, anyone proposing a toast, the first dance, bride's dad & bride dancing, groom's mom and groom dancing, etc. If friends are servers, get pictures of all of them, also with the bride and groom. Try to get pictures of all the guests. On such a busy day, the happy couple won't be able to remember who was there. Look through bridal magazines for other ideas.

Home Photo Shoots

For home photo shoots (using film), your client must understand that you cannot give them 24 great photos. It *could* happen, but the chances are good that it won't. If you are taking pictures of an active two year old, it is more difficult to get "perfect" pictures. Ask the parents what they want. Some want only perfectly posed pictures while others like photos that show their child's own unique personality.

Babies & Toddlers

Everyone wants good pictures of their new baby. Make a nice flyer and call on local hospitals to ask if you can put your info in their new mom package). Hand out your flyer at daycare facilities and preschools. Some preschools offer photo packages to parents.

For babies, use your imagination and try to look at as many other photos as possible for ideas. Go to the library and look at baby and new parent magazines. You might find some good tips at www.kodak.com.

One of my favorite shots was the blanket shot: baby must be old enough to hold its head up. Put baby on stomach and almost cover with *lightweight* blanket. Baby will hold head up, and *snap!* You have a precious peek-a-boo photo.

For toddlers, have a few props. A long feather duster is frequently effective. You can try it on the child, but the child is more likely to laugh if you tickle mommy with it. Have a silly hat, perhaps a hand puppet, and something that makes a funny noise. Some children are more comfortable when they are holding a favorite toy – a great memory photo.

Christmas Photos

Advertise for "Photos in Your Home" (their home) for holiday pictures. It is sometimes hard for a mom or dad to get a good photo of their own children. The kids will behave better for a stranger or someone who isn't in the immediate family.

For family portraits, use your "soft focus" or portrait lens for this shot. It will blur the tree lights ever so slightly and is an excellent look.

Animals
Animals can be tough to photograph because of the "red-eye" problem; however, the editing technology available should correct most of that. Whether using an SLR or digital camera, practice is the best way to learn. Photograph your own animals and offer to photograph your friends' animals – for free. But make sure you have everyone sign a release for the pictures. (Check online for free photo release forms.) You might get so many adorable shots that you could either put together a calendar yourself or sell your pictures to a calendar and/or greeting card company!

WRITING A THANK YOU NOTE
Thank you notes are important because they let the sender know you actually received what was sent and, most important, that their kindness was appreciated. The samples below are basic ideas, but always feel free to add more. Close relatives and family friends appreciate a personal note about what is going on in your life. Especially if you receive a generous check, you should send a longer, more personal thank you note.

Samples:
#1 *Dear Aunt Mary,*
Thank you so much for the slippers. They are a perfect fit, and I love that shade of blue. My feet will stay toasty warm this winter, and I will think of you each time I wear them! It was so sweet of you to remember me in such a nice way. (Or – It was so nice of you to remember me in such a lovely way.)
Again, thank you so very much for your thoughtfulness.

#2 *Dear Aunt Mary,*
Thank you so much for the graduation check. I am so excited about going to college and am looking forward to decorating my new dorm room. (Add some personal info here – some items you want to buy, classes you will be taking, etc.)
It was so nice of you to remember me in such a thoughtful way.

#3 *Dear Aunt Mary,*
Thank you so much for the baby shawl and sleepers. The shawl is absolutely beautiful and will be the perfect christening blanket. You have always had the knack for selecting the most wonderful gifts, and this one will always be treasured.
The sleepers are exactly what the baby needs for the cold winter nights ahead. I will think of you each time I dress Sarah for bed in those precious outfits!
Again, thank you so very much for your generosity and thoughtfulness.

INDEX

Dear Reader,

Thank you for taking time to read *"The Women's Survival Guide."* I sincerely hope you found it to be helpful in many ways – that it has given you some answers, ideas, hope, and a few laughs. My primary goals in writing this book were to inspire confidence in those who might be struggling – whether in personal relationships or financially – and to motivate those who are ready to make changes.

Over the years, I have met many people who struggle with a variety of problems. We have laughed together and cried together as we've swapped stories about good and bad times. Especially during times of challenge, it is important to know we are not the only ones with problems. Sometimes we just need a boost to help us turn things around or to see things in a different way. I hope you have found inspiration within these pages.

You are welcome to contact me with questions or comments. (Positive comments are preferred!) My website is www.lisacreedon.com.

Again, thank you so much for your interest.

Warmest wishes,

Lisa